# THE PORNOGRAPHY INDUSTRY

## WHAT EVERYONE NEEDS TO KNOW®

# THE PORNOGRAPHY INDUSTRY

## WHAT EVERYONE NEEDS TO KNOW®

### SHIRA TARRANT

OXFORD
UNIVERSITY PRESS

# OXFORD
UNIVERSITY PRESS

Oxford University Press is a department of the University of Oxford. It furthers
the University's objective of excellence in research, scholarship, and education
by publishing worldwide.Oxford is a registered trade mark of Oxford University
Press in the UK and certain other countries.

"What Everyone Needs to Know" is a registered trademark of  Oxford
University Press.

Published in the United States of America by Oxford University Press
198 Madison Avenue, New York, NY 10016, United States of America.

Library of Congress Cataloging-in-Publication Data
Names: Tarrant, Shira, 1963- author.
Title: The pornography industry : what everyone needs to
know / Shira Tarrant.
Description: First edition. | New York, NY :
Oxford University Press, [2016]
| Series: What everyone needs to know |
Includes bibliographical
references and index. | Description based on print version
record and CIP
data provided by publisher; resource not viewed.
Identifiers: LCCN 2015044219 (print) | LCCN 2015041007 (ebook) | ISBN
978–0–19–020514–0 (Epub) | ISBN 978–0–19–020513–3 (Updf) |
ISBN 978–0–19–020511–9
(hardcover : alk. paper) | ISBN 978–0–19–020512–6 (pbk. : alk. paper)
Subjects: LCSH: Pornography. | Pornographic film industry.
Classification: LCC HQ471 (print) | LCC HQ471 .T295 2016 (ebook) | DDC
363.4/7—dc23

LC record available at http://lccn.loc.gov/2015044219

1 3 5 7 9 8 6 4 2
Printed by RR Donnelley, USA

# CONTENTS

# ACKNOWLEDGMENTS

My editor Angela Chnapko deserves a great deal of thanks for answering my questions and providing feedback along the way. You've helped make the process of writing this book a pleasure. Thank you, Angela and Dave McBride, for bringing me on board with Oxford University Press. The copy editing expertise provided by Deanna Hegle and the skills of production editor Prabhu Chinnasamy made this book more precise. My thanks and appreciation also go to Lynn Comella for offering hot leads and a sounding board about porn and other controversial politics. Jiz Lee, Tristan Taormino, Adam Grayson, Brian Gross, April Flores, and Kevin Moore took the time to provide important insider info. Thank you! And of course, to my family: I extend my deep gratitude for your support and selective feedback as I continue on my adventures—academic and otherwise. I love you. You know who you are.

# INTRODUCTION

*The Pornography Industry: What Everyone Needs to Know* addresses key issues and concerns about a controversial and very hot topic. This book will appeal to a curious and intelligent audience who wants to know about the foundations and development of this popular and sometimes reviled pop culture genre. Gone are the days when finding porn meant going to a red-light district, an X-rated movie theater, or receiving a snail-mail package in discreet brown paper wrapping. Today, pornography is no further away than a smartphone, tablet, or a laptop. Pornography's ubiquity and easy access makes the subject timely and important. Like any issue reshaping our cultural landscape, pornography deserves discussion. Yet, despite its widespread use, people are generally more at ease using porn secretly than they are likely to talk about it openly. This contributes to misinformation and taboo around sexuality, neither of which is safe, smart, or advisable. Given that it is often (and understandably) easier for people to privately watch porn than to publicly talk about it, this book is intended to provide fact-based information that adds to readers' comfort levels in considering the questions and understanding what may be at stake.

To that end, topics in this book include the history of pornography, legal issues, medical research, social affairs, and political debates. In the chapters that follow, I will also explain the industry basics—who works in porn; how much they earn; rapid technological changes that are shaping production, distribution, and user access; along with often-elusive revenue data.

Although why people like porn may seem obvious, there are important topics to consider: How many kids have access to porn? Should we be concerned about teen viewers? Is pornography racist and sexist? Does porn cause harm or violence toward women? Can people become addicted to porn? Is watching porn the same as infidelity?

I have aimed to address these political debates and competing perspectives regarding pornography in an even-handed manner, giving equal time to various sides of the arguments. In *The Pornography Industry*, I survey important legal and cultural issues emerging around the globe while focusing specifically on case law, legislation, trends, and topics in the United States.

Although myths and misinformation are plentiful, accurate data is deeply needed. The following chapters are researched based and avoid moral or political judgment to provide a trustworthy source for rational information. The goal of this book is to provide the most current and reliable scholarship available to help make sense of the provocative, contentious, and sometimes high-stakes issues at hand. It will be up to you, the reader, to make your own best decisions when it comes to the politics and pleasures of porn.

# 1

# OVERVIEW

## *What Is the Definition of Pornography?*

In 1964, the Supreme Court of the United States faced a controversy over whether Louis Malle's French film *The Lovers* violated the First Amendment prohibition against obscene speech. In determining what exactly distinguishes pornography from obscenity, Justice Potter Stewart famously said that perhaps he could never succeed in precisely defining porn. But he went on to say, "I know it when I see it."

In *Jacobellis v. Ohio*, the case about the Malle film that prompted Stewart's comment, the Court ruled in favor of Nico Jacobellis, manager of the Coventry Neighborhood Heights Art Theatre in Cleveland Heights. But while, in this instance, the Court overturned Jacobellis's previous obscenity conviction, handed down by the Supreme Court of Ohio, the controversy and debates continue over how to define pornography.

In general, *pornography* refers to visual depictions that are intended to sexually arouse the viewer, such as still photos, magazines, adult cable television channels, or VHS movies. Today, pornography is more likely to mean online video; and, in the future, technological changes may again shift how these visual depictions are delivered to the consumer.

But regardless of the medium, the challenge in defining the term is that one person's pornography may seem like hate speech to the next person or like nothing at all to a third. What arouses a plushy, for instance, may go unnoticed by someone without a sexual interest in cute stuffed animals. Whereas some think of the *Victoria's Secret* catalogue as reference information about lingerie and sale prices, others find it a rich source of masturbatory material. Depending on one's political perspective, some may even think that music videos, romance novels, or fiction such as *Fifty Shades of Grey* are pornographic. So what is the distinction between pornography and erotica—or even unintentionally erotic material that is used for sexual gratification? And how can we tell the difference?

### What Is the Difference between Erotica and Porn?

Much like there are debates over the definition of what constitutes pornography, there is no hard and fast definition for erotica. In general, *erotica* is considered "softer," or less explicit, than XXX-rated, or hard-core, material. In his 1966 research on Victorian smut, literary scholar Steven Marcus drew a distinction between erotic literature, which has multiple intentions, and pornography, which has only one. Lacking a clear definition or legal guidelines, the question deciding what is erotic—much like art or beauty—is left to the eye of the beholder.

Anti-porn feminists argue that pornography reflects patriarchal hegemony in which one person is oppressing or abusing the other, while erotica depicts sex among equals and is thus free of subjugation. Gloria Steinem is quoted as saying that pornography is about dominance, but erotica is about mutuality. While Steinem's point is that pornography's "lethal confusion of sex with violence" is dangerous for women, film critic and cultural critic B. Ruby Rich argues that an element of judgment drives the argument: "If I like it, it's erotic; if you like it, it's pornographic."[1]

Some turn to etymology to resolve the debate, but even here the matter is murky. One account holds that the ancient Greek *porne* refers to whores and the term *graphos* means describing. A somewhat different spin on the translation claims that *pornographos* means writing by prostitutes, not about them. In contrast, the ancient Greek *eros*, the root of the word erotica, means passion or love. An erotic book or movie may be defined today as content that contains a storyline or a plot. However, this does not prevent controversy, as exemplified by debates over whether *Fifty Shades of Grey* portrays life-affirming erotica or pornographic abuse.

Unlike erotica, mere use of the word pornography can evoke negative reactions and harsh political backlash. For example, classifying visual representations as pornographic has been used to justify legal restrictions to information about homosexuality in some countries, or even to prosecute gay businesses. To sidestep the vagueness of the term "erotica," the negative bias that can accompany the term "pornography," and to avoid the suggestion that sexual images are inherently negative, some instead prefer the term "adult entertainment" or "visual sexual stimuli" (VSS) in referring to visual representations that are likely to provoke a sexual response.

Clearly, the criteria are arbitrary for defining the difference between erotica and porn, and debate over the terms continues today.

### Why Does Pornography Matter?

Like all genres of pop culture, it is easy to dismiss pornography as "just entertainment," not containing any "real" significance or impact. When it comes to pornography, it can be even easier to dismiss the entire genre as mere jack-off material. Yet it is precisely this dismissal that renders pop culture—and specifically pornography—so crucial to understand. Its ubiquitous presence in so many aspects of our lives means that pornography is a rich source for studying the ways in which ideas about gender, race, class, beauty, and sex are constructed, conveyed, and maintained. Pornography is an important media category for questioning normative expectations and exploring forms of resistance that challenge racism, classism, ageism, and related intersectional subjugations. Pornography has been at the center of legislation, lawsuits, and public debate. It is the site where legal controversy over free speech and censorship collide. Pornography impacts both public politics and private life.

As a legitimate subject of study, however, pornography has been, until relatively recently, dismissed as lowbrow, silly, or as meaningless fluff. For some, pornography is simply too embarrassing to study and discuss. This makes it even more important to study and analyze the unquestioned power that popular or mass culture exerts on our collective and individual imaginations.

Pornography can be understood as a sociological phenomenon that provides a glimpse into historical and contemporary morés, fashion, politics, and trends. In a democracy, freedom of expression is foundational to other privileges of social citizenship such as liberty, justice, agency, self-definition, and visibility. Because pornography invokes these issues—whether in the courtroom or in the court of public opinion—this genre has the potential to impact matters that are central to social citizenship and everyday life. Finally, understanding pornography is important because information about media creates and encourages a stronger ability to distinguish between fantasy and reality, yes and no, coercion and consent—lines that can be fuzzy in porn and in real life. The more we understand the pornography industry, the better situated we are to know the difference.

### Is Pornography a Crime, a Sin, a Vice, or a Choice?

Depending on whom you ask, and the type of pornography in question, the answer might be any or all of the preceding. Child pornography is unequivocally illegal in most countries and falls under the jurisdiction of Interpol and specific national governments. The legal status of simulated child porn, however, varies around the globe. Then there are some

perhaps surprising legal distinctions in regard to pornographic content. For instance, in Poland, producing zoo porn
is illegal while owning it for personal use is not; in Singapore,
it is legal to watch pornography online but against the law to
supply or to download it; in 2012, Gaza's Hamas government
began blocking access to sexually explicit websites. Several
US states, Israel, Germany, and the Australian state of Victoria
have passed laws making revenge porn a crime; but international standards are inconsistent.

Because the Internet involves transnational trade and com-
munication, whether or not distributing, buying, or possessing Internet porn is a crime for the most part depends on local
laws. In other words, even if a company legally distributes
porn, it may not be legal for a person to receive it.

In regard to whether pornography is a vice, again, this
depends on culture, religion, and context. There are sects of
every major religion that consider pornography to be a vice
or a sin. Conservative Christian doctrine warns that pornography leads to the "deadly sin of lust and the mortal sin of
masturbation." Some Christians consider pornography a form
of adultery, which is forbidden in the Bible. Judaism does not
oppose erotica, but orthodox and conservative groups promote modesty, which is rather the antithesis of porn. The
United Methodist Church emphasizes that pornography
degrades, exploits, and coerces. Pornography directly conflicts
with Islamic teachings that promote self-control; looking at the
private parts of another person who is not one's husband or
wife is considered an ethical violation. According to data from
the Public Religion Research Institute, however, a 69 percent
majority of Americans claim that watching porn is morally
acceptable. Civil libertarians and apolitical people may consider pornography simply as a matter of personal choice and
free will. Clearly, these are complicated and contested positions, and I will address them more directly in the chapters
that follow.

## *If Pornography Is a Private Issue, Why Talk about It in Public?*

Pornography cuts to the heart of sexual pleasure, sexual danger, censorship, free speech, coercion, and personal agency. Joseph Slade explains in his book *Pornography in America* that because "arguments over sexual expression mask issues of politics, religion, gender, race, class and (above all) sexuality, irrelevant claims and assertions are not merely typical but seemingly essential to any discussion of pornography. At times, the confusion seems a deliberate means of demonizing enemies, achieving political advantage, or making a profit."[2]

Then there is the unease about pornography as a source of sex education and how, lacking better resources, teens and young adults may learn about relationships primarily from porn. Actor and activist Jane Fonda points out in her 2014 book, *Being a Teen*, that there is a risk of "learning from porn how to be in a sexual relationship, what is sexy, how to look and act." Because of legislation that prevents or limits comprehensive sex education in public schools, pornography is often the main source of sexual information for teens (and adults). According to the Guttmacher Institute, as of March 2014, twenty-two states and the District of Columbia mandate that public schools teach sex education. Of those, only thirteen states require that sex education content must be "medically, factually or technically accurate." Because accurate information is the key to sexual pleasure, health, and safety, it is all the more important to understand pornography in politically astute and media-literate ways.

The quantitative evidence supports this concern. Between 1988 and 2005, there was a tenfold increase in the number of porn videos produced (13,000 vs. 1,300).[3] Yet a survey of teenagers conducted by *Psychologies* magazine found that during this same time period, 75 percent of parents never talked with their children about pornography. The Kaiser Family Foundation finds that as these teens become adults, few take seriously the idea that marketing is a force from which they must take hold of creativity, individuality, and autonomy. This creates generations that are not given the tools to think critically about both sexuality and the role of media in their lives. With the steady availability of pornography, this educational oversight becomes both a personal and a public health matter.

### What Makes Pornography a Valence Issue?

Responses to pornography can range from revulsion to compulsion, from animosity to excitement. Like other sexually related issues, pornography tends to evoke strong emotions and visceral responses. This is because sexuality is a core part of forming our identities and our communities. In the field of psychology, *emotional valence* refers to topics that evoke a strong emotional response. These emotions can be negative or positive; but either way, these feelings are strong.

Generally speaking, a city council proposal to plant new grass in the parks, for instance, is unlikely to yield outrage or picketing, or even an online petition of support. There are many other equally unremarkable matters in daily politics and everyday life that don't register on the emotional scale. Pornography is more likely to be a valence issue. This is especially true if there are matters of morality, sexual orientation, gender and trans status, or race and ethnicity at hand. This is the case historically, globally, and currently. Religion, morals, debates about agency, free speech, and free will—combined with the most intimate experiences of sexual desire and pleasure—converge to create what are often heated emotional responses to pornography. There are concerns about children's access to porn and, with indisputable good reason, concerns about child porn. Debate over mandatory condom use on the set of porn shoots has yielded robust, often impassioned, debate.

In the field of political science, however, the concept of valence issues is defined a bit differently from the field of psychology. For political scientists, a *valence issue* is one with which the community usually shares a common preference.

Voters are likely to uniformly reject corruption in govern-ment; residents want their communities to prosper. Opinions can become divided when it comes to deciding how corrup-tion should be punished or which political party is more likely to actually promote prosperity. Political scientists refer to the focus of these divided viewpoints as "position issues." People tend to have strong emotional responses to pornography and differing ideas about what, if anything at all, should be done to address it. In this sense, pornography can be considered a psychological valence issue and a politically positional one.

# 2

# HISTORICAL QUESTIONS

## When Did Pornography Begin?

Since ancient civilizations, people have created explicit depictions of sex and nudity. This erotica was often intertwined with religious or supernatural ideas about sexuality and included artwork, artifacts, music, murals, and poetry. Paleolithic cave paintings included nudes and human genitalia dating back to more than 2.6 million years ago. The Turin Erotic Papyrus was an ancient scroll painted during Egypt's Ramesside period (1292–1075 BCE), two-thirds of which includes explicit depictions of sexual acts. The Roman city of Pompeii had frescoes that included people having sex. Latin poets produced work frankly describing sex and desire. The *Kama Sutra* is an ancient Hindu text from India that includes poetry, prose, advice, and illustrations as guidelines for sexual behavior, erotic love, and gracious living. Sappho's *Hymn to Aphrodite* (600 BCE) is one of the earliest examples of lesbian erotic poetry. Among the many other pieces of early erotic art and literature are the Peruvian pottery of the Moche people (100 CE to 800 CE); *The Perfumed Garden of Sensual Delight*, a fifteenth-century Arabic sex manual; and Japanese erotic woodblock prints and paintings called *Shunga*, which date back to the ninth century and were produced in large numbers between the 1600s and the 1900s but originated in China several centuries earlier.

Despite the historical existence of graphic sexuality in art, religion, and literature, these are not necessarily pornographic. These examples may be explicit and arousing, but they were created in a cultural context that celebrated nudity in ways that contemporary cultures often find embarrassing, shameful, or even taboo. Using historian Lynn Hunt's definition, pornography contains particular elements. Paraphrasing her description from *The Invention of Pornography: Obscenity and the Origins of Modernity*, Hunt explains that porn includes (a) written or visual representation of sexual behavior or sexualized body parts, with (b) an intentional violation of widely accepted moral and social taboos, and (c) an objective to arouse sexual feelings. Using Hunt's framework, pornography (for the most part) has only existed since around the 1600s.

### How Has Pornography Changed over Time?

With the rise of Christianity, cultural and religious outlooks on nudity and sexuality began to change compared with prior eras. The New Testament emphasized procreative sex between husband and wife, thus establishing any other sexual expression as an evil violation of the Bible. Nonetheless, artists of the Renaissance continued to produce renowned material such as Agnolo Bronzino's painting of a nude Cupid, fondling the breast of an also-nude Venus, and kissing his mother on the mouth. The amount of sexually explicit literature grew so large during this era that the Catholic Church issued the Index Librorum Prohibitorum, a list of all the publications a Catholic should not read. But even the Church contained erotic art. As journalist Debbie Nathan comments in her book *Pornography*, the blend of explicit imagery and Biblical prohibition must have no doubt been a mixed message. (The Catholic Church abolished the Index Librorum Prohibitorum in 1966.)

The Marquis de Sade (1740–1814), a French aristocrat, was infamously considered a sexual libertine by some, a moral pornographer by others, and a sexual abuser by yet others. De Sade is best known for his erotic writing that includes violent sexual fantasies, along with political philosophy and his disdain for the Catholic Church. The words "sadism" and "sadist" are derived from his name. Among de Sade's most well-known work includes *The 120 Days of Sodom, or the School of Libertinism* (written in 1785; published in 1904); *Philosophy in the Bedroom* (1795); and *Juliette* (1797), a novel about an amoral nymphomaniac murderer, which includes violent pornographic scenes blended with philosophical and theological treatises. Some experts even suggest that de Sade's books were actually political invectives disguised as pornography.

By the 1700s, novels were becoming a popular form of literature and often highlighted overtly sexual themes. With the invention of the steam-powered rotary printing press in the 1800s, books were far easier to publish. Among the better-known European works of pornography or erotica from the Victorian era (1837–1901) are *The Pearl*, a magazine of short stories and poems that was published from 1879 to 1881; Alfred de Musset's *Gamiani, or Two Nights of Excess* (1870); and *Venus in Furs* by Leopold von Sacher-Masoch (1870) from whom the word *masochism* gets its meaning.

*The Sins of the Cities of the Plain* (1881), written under the pseudonym "Jack Saul," is one of the first English-language publications of pornographic literature featuring exclusively gay male sex. *Sins of the Cities of the Plain* traces the sexual awakening of Jack, a young male prostitute, and is written as a series of confessional essays. Jack's initial innocence is introduced by coy passages such as "I believe that idea quite daft, a bum is for droppings and was never constructed to do otherwise." This is followed a few pages later with Jack screaming, "Slap my arse; bugger me; shove your prick into me as I fuck him!" *Vice* magazine reports that the book "was written by two real-life Victorian transvestites who were part of a gay brothel ring that Prince Albert Victor used to frequent." Read by Oscar Wilde, *Sins* reportedly inspired the famous pornographic gay literature, *Teleny, or the Reverse of the Medal*, which was first published in London in 1893 and attributed to Wilde, although his authorship is disputed.

Much of the famous erotic literature from the Victorian Era is graphic and bold, even by the assumptions that today's standards are more liberal. *Romance of Lust*, written by Anonymous, was originally published in four volumes between 1873 and 1876. It describes in graphic detail themes of incest, homosexuality, and orgies. *My Secret Life* (1888–1894) and *Forbidden Fruit* (1898) also feature fetish and taboo subjects including sadomasochism and cross-generational sex. Mark Twain's *1601* features scatological fare including sexual misadventures and fairly detailed fictional accounts of famous writers discussing their farts. It is even more scandalous because *1601* is written as if it comes from the diary of one of Queen Elizabeth I's ladies-in-waiting. As a result of obscenity accusations, many of these works were banned until the 1960s. Salacious sexual literature from the Victorian era was often published anonymously or under pen names. Mark Twain (itself a pseudonym for Samuel Clemens) never admitted he was the author of *1601* until twenty years after the pamphlet was published in 1880. This is perhaps ironic given Twain's critical stance on political duplicity.

As sexually explicit novels and newly available pornographic moving images flourished during the Victorian Era, so did claims that masturbating drove people ill, insane, or blind. As the century progressed, so did a putatively scientific backlash against masturbation. The wealthy class believed that the men among them were rational enough to handle this sort of material, but the rich worried that the lower classes would stop working productively if they were distracted by adult-themed material. In 1857, England passed a law forbidding the sale and distribution of obscene materials. By the end of the century, boys or girls caught masturbating were often forced into chastity devices that prevented them from touching their own genitals or "cures" that involved electrical shock. One "treatment" even involved the application of carbolic acid to the clitoris.

During this same era, physicians believed that a variety of emotional and physical conditions were linked to women's reproductive systems. Women with headaches, melancholy, aggression, depression, abdominal heaviness, muscle pains, and other general discomfort were diagnosed with "female hysteria," derived from the ancient Greek idea of a "wandering womb seeking its proper place." Victorian Era physicians treated women with this so-called medical condition by stimulating the genitals of their female patients. This produced what they called "hysterical paroxysm," more commonly known today as an orgasm. As Rachel P. Maines explains in *The Technology of Orgasm*, this medical treatment led to the invention of the vibrator in 1869 by George Taylor, MD, as a labor-saving device for physicians treating afflicted women.

### How Has Technology Impacted Pornography?

Media scholar Kevin Heffernan writes that the unsexy topics of economics and distribution have an ongoing impact on how pornography is created and made available to the public.[1] The relative difficulty or ease with which pornography is made available—and to whom—has effects on laws, morés, and other aspects of sexual politics. Like more recent advances, early, relatively low-tech developments in production and distribution, such as the invention of the printing press or the still camera, impacted the quantity, content, and availability of pornography.

By the mid-1700s, the novel was becoming a popular form of literature, including those books with explicitly sexual storylines. *Fanny Hill: Memoirs of a Woman of Pleasure,* written by John Cleland and initially published in 1748, is one well-known example. *Fanny Hill* is considered the first instance of pornography produced in novel form. The story blends class politics with sexual pursuit. But with its prostitute protagonist, *Fanny*'s main appeal has been the sex, specifically because the book includes voyeurism, orgies, bisexuality, and masochism. Originally published in England, it was quickly renounced by the court. It also quickly became a bestseller in Europe, and by 1820, pirated copies were being smuggled into the United States.

When Richard M. Hoe invented the steam-powered rotary printing press in 1843, it became possible to produce millions of copies of a page in one day. This meant larger production and thus easier availability of pamphlets and books. The pulp magazines that became popular between roughly 1896 and 1955 included the soft-core porn genre known as saucy and spicy. These magazines featured titles such as *Wink: A Whirl of Girls*, *Flirt: A FRESH Magazine*, and *Snappy*. Standard cover stories included features such as "bare facts of burlesque," "perky pin-ups," or "high-heel cuties." The magazines were usually sold from under the counter.

When photography was invented, some of the first photos ever made included nudity and sex. Almost immediately after Louis Daguerre invented the daguerreotype in 1839, pornographers appropriated the new technology. The earliest surviving example dates back to about 1846 and depicts "a rather solemn man gingerly inserting his penis into the vagina of an equally solemn and middle-aged woman."[2] Similarly, when cinema was developed in the late 1800s, some of these first moving images also depicted people having sex.

In 1889, Thomas Edison invented the movie camera and movie projector. By 1895, William Dickson, Edison's former assistant, branched out on his own to invent the mutoscope, a hand-cranked flipbook. The most popular reel shown was titled *What the Butler Saw*, which was effectively the first peep show in history.

In 1896, Eugène Pirou and Albert Kirchner produced the first pornographic movies. These early films usually portrayed relatively mild situations such as women bathing or getting dressed, but these relatively tame features rapidly shifted.

Between 1907 and 1915, porn became notably more explicit. Film studies scholar Linda Williams comments that the movies of this era often featured genital close-ups and medium-range camera angles of sex acts, both of which are styles far more similar to more contemporary porn films than those prior to these dates.

*L'Ecu d'Or ou la Bonne Auberge,* a French film made in 1908, is the oldest surviving porn film that can be accurately dated. The plot featured a tryst between a soldier and a servant girl at an inn. By 1910, the German film *Am Abend* included voyeurism, masturbation, fellatio, and various styles of heterosexual intercourse including a close-up "master shot" at the end of the movie. This change in film style and plot intensity is interesting on its own; but, as Heffernan explains, changes in distribution have specifically major effects on the aesthetic styles of adult films including generic norms, camera techniques, and even the "porn star" system. Key censorship struggles faced by the contemporary adult industry also appear after major changes in modes of distribution. And, with each change in porn distribution methods, new sets of practices in the business follow. Producers, distributors, exhibitors, retailers, performers, and websites all attempt to standardize trade practices after distribution moves into a new phase. The adult industry trade press, political lobbying groups, publicity and promotion efforts, industry awards, and the visibility of industry figures among mainstream media are also impacted by changing distribution practices.

In relatively more recent decades, technological changes in production and distribution can be parsed into the following eras: the stag films that appeared in the early twentieth century, porn loops distributed to peep-show booths in the 1960s, and the theatrically released feature films of the so-called golden era of the 1970s. In the 1980s, with the ascendance of home video, adult film's theatrical distribution declined and the video era dawned.

### How Did Porn Evolve in the Twentieth Century?

Some of the most famous erotic novels of the twentieth century include Georges Bataille's *Story of the Eye* (1928); *Tropic of Cancer* (1934) and *Tropic of Capricorn* (1938) by Henry Miller; and the French *Histoire d'O* (*Story of O*), a tale of a woman's sexual submission, published in 1954 under the pen name Pauline Réage. The book was actually written by Anne Cécile Desclos, initially as a collection of letters to her real-life lover, Jean Paulhan.

Anaïs Nin originally wrote the short stories that comprise *Delta of Venus* for a private patron in the 1940s. The fifteen collected pieces were published in 1977, after Nin's death. Anaïs Nin also wrote the thirteen short stories that compose *Little Birds* in the 1940s as part of a group of writers who wrote porn for pay at a daily rate of one dollar. *Little Birds* was published posthumously in 1979 as a collected volume.

During World War II, innocent yet seductive pin-up art became popular, launching to fame models and actresses such as Jane Russell, Veronica Lake, Rita Hayworth, and the Vargas and Elvgren Girls. These images were sent to the troops overseas and sometimes even painted on aircraft to help bolster morale and militarism. In 1955, the legendary Bettie Page was awarded the title "Miss Pinup Girl of the World"; and by the mid-twentieth century, Hugh Hefner, Bob Guccione, and Larry Flynt published the first issues of *Playboy* (1953), *Penthouse* (1965), and *Hustler* (1979), respectively.

When Marilyn Monroe appeared as the first *Playboy* centerfold, her image created a stir for being risqué. However, the glossy men's magazine never showed photographs of pubic hair or genitals in the early days. *Playboy* billed itself as an upscale periodical, and Hugh Hefner described the magazine as a "handbook for the urban male." Along with photos of naked women, each issue included articles and interviews about politics and culture with features by luminaries such as Joseph Heller, Gabriel García Márquez, Margaret Atwood, Haruki Murakami, and Kurt Vonnegut. Ray Bradbury's novel

*Fahrenheit 451* initially appeared as serialized stories in early issues of *Playboy* in 1954. Because *Playboy* was so well known for its famous contributors, a long-standing joke was that people "read it for the articles."

In 1963, feminist icon Gloria Steinem famously worked undercover as a bunny in a Manhattan Playboy Club to write a two-part article for *Show* magazine exposing the financial exploitation and institutionalized male sexism. Despite the attention garnered by Steinem's exposé, *Playboy* was so popular that it became the first adult magazine to be printed in Braille, beginning in 1970 under the National Library Service for the Blind and Physically Handicapped. Yet for all of *Playboy's* popularity and its putatively high-class clubs, *Penthouse* had a racier appeal: the nude photos of women in *Penthouse* included pubic hair.

*Penthouse* was first published in 1965 in the United Kingdom, and by September 1969, *Penthouse* was sold in the United States as well. Speaking to *New York Magazine* in 2004, *Penthouse* founder Bob Guccione told reporter Anthony Haden-Guest, "We were the first to show full frontal nudity. The first to expose the clitoris completely. I think we made a very serious contribution to the liberalization of laws and attitudes. [Television cable station] HBO would not have gone as far as it does if it wasn't for us breaking the barriers. Much that has happened now in the Western world with respect to sexual advances is directly due to steps that we took."

Within a year after *Penthouse* broke boundaries by showing women's pubic hair, *Playboy* began showing slight wisps as well. This competition among the best-selling adult magazines was referred to as the Pubic Wars, a play on the ancient Punic Wars between Rome and Carthage. Of course, any claim to victory in the so-called Pubic Wars began changing in the 1980s when fashion dictated that models feature a partially trimmed "bush." Over time, this trend changed again when full bikini waxes came into vogue.

*Penthouse* was popular with people who wanted more explicit photographs than *Playboy* showed, but this race to be most explicit was overshadowed when Larry Flynt started publishing *Hustler*.

*Hustler* went where no mass-market porn magazine had gone before. Its pages featured female genitals, sex acts, fetishes, and sex toys. Whereas pubic hair appeared for the first time in *Penthouse* in 1970, *Hustler* pushed things further by publishing the first labial "pink shots" in 1974. *Hustler* was billed as a working-class alternative to the urbane profile of *Playboy* and *Penthouse*; but it promoted a crass, sexist imagery that, for many, simply crossed a line.

At around the same time as glossy men's magazines were gaining in popularity, Helen Gurley Brown, then-editor of *Cosmopolitan*, ran a 1972 centerfold featuring actor Burt Reynolds in the nude, a pose that has since been emulated by famous actors, politicians, and ad campaigns. *Cosmo's* success also spawned *Playgirl* in 1973. The magazine was ostensibly geared toward heterosexual women by featuring nude males, but it also attracted a significant gay male readership. Like the evolving appearance of female pubic hair in adult magazines, researchers in a 2000 issue of the *International Journal of Eating Disorders* reported that among the 115 male centerfold models in *Playgirl* magazine from 1973 to 1997, physiques became increasingly dense and more muscular over time. This evidence points to the fact that aesthetic standards of gender and beauty change over time and across cultures, and this is reflected in pornography just like other media.

### What Are Stag Films?

The original stag films were not only transgressive; in the United States, they were completely outlawed. Still, stag films remained popular from 1900 until at least 1940. "Stag"—meaning "men only"—referred to the all-male homosocial groups who watched these films together.

Early stag films were silent, black and white, and were on average twelve minutes long. Joseph W. Slade explains that based on the approximately 1,000 surviving stag films, we know the content included hard-core scenes of intercourse, masturbation, penetration with objects, and other scenes focused on the genitals. In Germany, France, and the United States, stag films were screened in all-male locations, not in mainstream theaters. Many of these early European film screenings took place in secret cinemas and rarely operated from the same place twice. The underground locations were fiercely guarded secrets, and because these screenings were illegal, information was generally not released until as close to the event time as possible. Brothels were frequently used to screen stag films, often with female sex workers present to showcase the talent and specialized services offered by the hosting establishment. The brothel location of stag screenings and the economic incentive function they served helps to explain the high production value and what Heffernan describes as "the performers' unusually wide sexual repertoire."

Stag films often featured burlesque or full-length features with women teasing and flirting with the viewer as opposed to overt demonstrations of sex. *Le Menage Moderne du Madame Butterfly* (controversially attributed to Bernard Natan, c. 1920) is the first known film to depict bisexual and homosexual acts. *A Free Ride* or *Grass Sandwich* (c. 1915) is classic stag film from the silent era and is thought to be among the earliest examples of American hard-core porn. In short, the plot involves a male motorist who picks up two women at the side of the road, after which a threesome ensues. Many of these early films are among the collections at the Kinsey Institute for Research in Sex, Gender, and Reproduction in Bloomington, Indiana.

In the 1960s, after porn was legalized in several European countries, short, hard-core, 8 mm films boomed, and adult magazines became available for export to retail shops in American cities. When the number of adult bookstores increased in the late 1960s, several firms started leasing 8 mm viewing booths that stores installed for patrons to privately watch these short, hard-core films. Soon after, short film loops became hugely popular. These loops were made from splicing films so they could run through a projector repeatedly without having to pause for a reel change. In the United States, semi-underground production of porn films flourished. These modest-scale productions were often released as low-quality, silent, black-and-white loops for the peep-show booths in adult video arcades, especially those found around New York City's Times Square.

### What Is the Golden Era of Porn?

In 1960, about twenty adult movie theaters began opening in the Western United States. Over the next decade, more than 750 X-rated theaters opened across the country. In 1970, *Mona the Virgin Nymph* became the first adult movie with a plot to receive wide release in movie theaters. This marked the beginning of the golden era of porn, or what's known as porno chic. Adult movies from this era had theatrical releases and relatively high production values, and they enjoyed a brief period of mainstream popularity.

When *Deep Throat* came out in 1972, and *The Devil in Miss Jones* came out in 1973, it became trendy to watch X-rated porn films (or at least some) in public theaters. After Johnny Carson mentioned *Deep Throat* during his popular late-night TV show, celebrities, diplomats, businesspeople, and critics began flocking to theaters and discussing the phenomenon in mainstream media. *Deep Throat*'s surging popularity led *New York Times* journalist Ralph Blumenthal to describe the trend as "porno chic" in his January 1973 article subtitled "Hard-core grows fashionable—and very profitable." Within seven months of its premier on June 12, 1972, *Deep Throat* grossed over $3.2 million, was screened in more than 70 theaters across the country, and drew an average of 5,000 people a week to shows at the New Mature World Theater in Manhattan.

By the 1980s, video replaced film as the preferred medium in creating porn. Along with this change in production technique, high-value quality generally declined as more people made more porn more quickly—and often with low budgets. For this reason, the high-value period prior to video production is known as pornography's golden era.

### What Is the Video Era of Porn?

Home video was first introduced in Japan in 1975 with the release of Sony Betamax. Beta, as it was known, soon gave way to even newer technology.

In 1980, the home video cassette player (VCR) was invented. And in 1985, invention of the camcorder enabled users to record directly to VHS tapes. This meant that anyone with a camcorder could now make pornography. By the early 1980s, video was replacing loop reels in viewing booths and public arcades, but big budget films with major stars still had box office draw. Initially, video successfully coexisted with hardcore films in public theaters. Eventually, however, the ease and privacy of video supplanted film in popularity.

In the days of independent neighborhood video stores, customers could easily rent X-rated videos. There was an upsurge in the number of women renting pornography, presumably because access no longer meant going to a sex shop or to an X-rated theater in a questionable neighborhood.

The impact of new technology on porn use continued. By 2011, *The Wall Street Journal* was reporting that "the porn problem" was not its proliferation but, rather, that the number of customers using pay-per-view cable and satellite TV had dropped off precipitously in favor of the Internet. Time Warner Cable, for instance, released data showing that shrinkage in the adult category was responsible for a roughly $5 million decline in video-on-demand revenue. Although porn was only a very small portion of Time Warner's $4.9 billion quarterly revenue, it had been one of the television provider's most profitable segments: that is, until the technology significantly changed in the twenty-first century.

## What Is the Digital Era of Porn?

The digital era refers to the Internet and the invention of the digital camera. Both tech developments shifted the way pornography is made and watched. In the early days of the Internet, and prior to the World Wide Web, ASCII code was used to create porn online using characters to create explicit imagery of people, or symbols such as (o)(o) to represent a woman's breasts.

The ease of production, access, and the availability of an increasingly wider range of content has created an explosion of websites devoted to porn, a resurgence of debates about pornography's suggested harms and benefits, and an opportunism that has resulted in breaking more boundaries.

Adult sexual entertainment has historically included a range of genres from pottery to bawdy folklore to real-time webcam work. Sexual speech; erotic newspapers, magazines, comics, and literature; erotic art, live performance, film, electronic media, and Internet porn are all features of pornography. In the day of the stag film, watching porn was available primarily in brothels. During the golden era, watching porn meant going to an X-rated theater, most likely in a dicey neighborhood; and for many, this meant hoping nobody saw you go in. That was not a safe space for women. But access to high-speed, live-action visuals has changed things. The Internet makes it easier to access pornography. But technology has also changed the types of acts shown on-screen. The shift from illegal stag films to X-rated theaters to privately viewed Internet clips has impacted the types of sex acts shown on-screen. A 1994 Carnegie Mellon study of early porn use found that 48 percent of downloads depicted bestiality, incest, and pedophilia. Fewer than 5 percent of these downloads depicted vaginal sex.[3]

With laptops, high-speed Wi-Fi, cell phones, and newer technology, we can pretty much get porn anytime, anywhere. For better and worse, technology has arguably democratized access to pornography. In 1989, Linda Williams predicted that virtual reality would one day become a new permutation of pornography. As we will see in later chapters, this prediction was an astute one.

### What Is Some of the Most Famous (or Infamous) Porn in History?

Among the canon of famous or infamous porn are those that are known for their artistic vision, for pushing sociopolitical boundaries, violating social norms, bringing porn mainstream, or for instigating landmark legal cases. Although creating a comprehensive list of all the well-known porn throughout history would be an impossibly monumental project, there are specific movies worth mentioning, in addition to the material listed elsewhere in this chapter.

I Am Curious (Yellow), released in 1967—and its 1968 companion film, I Am Curious (Blue)—feature the same characters, cast, and crew. In short, the lead character is named Lena, a political activist who believes in pacifism and equality. During her encounters across Stockholm, Lena begins a love triangle and a passionate affair with a man named Börje. As a young woman of twenty, Lena is searching for understanding. In doing so, she chronicles all of her experiences, including her political activism and personal relationships. Written and directed by Vilgot Sjöman, both films are at once political and sexual; however, they have slightly different slants. Yellow emphasizes class consciousness and nonviolence, whereas Blue focuses on religion, prisons, and sex. I am Curious (Yellow) became immensely popular in the United States in part because it was the first porn film shown outside of porn theaters and therefore more comfortably accessible to a broader audience. According to the Sunday Times in London, the film was a box office hit, earning $6.6 million shortly after release. Yet the film was also highly controversial. It was seized by customs when the film first arrived in the United States due to nudity, including full frontal male nudity, and explicit sex.

In 1972, *Deep Throat*, directed by Gerard Damiano, and *Behind the Green Door* (Mitchell Brothers, 1972) became infamous for their explicit portrayals of sex and for the spectacle of their mainstream popularity during the porno chic era. Linda Lovelace and Marilyn Chambers were the respective stars of these two films, and both became household names. At about this same time, *The Devil in Miss Jones* (Gerard Damiano, 1973) was released. This porn film blends bold sexuality with psychological intrigue, exploring issues of lust and regret. The film features Georgina Spelvin playing Justine Jones, John Clemens as Abaca, and Harry Reems (born Herbert Streicher), playing The Teacher.

The story of "The Devil" is that Miss Jones is facing an eternity in hell because she has committed suicide, an act brought about because of despair over feeling that nothing has happened in her life. Although she's led an exemplary life, Abaca informs Miss Jones she is doomed to hell because she has killed herself. Upon hearing this news, she asks to briefly return to earth to earn her place in hell by pursuing one of the seven deadly sins: lust. The ensuing plot involves a series of encounters including sexual pain, group sex, lesbian sex, a python snake, a bathtub hose, and a bowl of fruit. The unsettling end of the film features Miss Jones' eternal punishment in hell— a lust that can never be satisfied. Despite its X rating by the MPAA, *The Devil in Miss Jones* outearned both *Deep Throat* and *Behind the Green Door*.

Viewers also flocked to theaters to see *Boys in the Sand* (Wakefield Poole, 1971). This movie was popular among gay and straight audiences, and was the first gay film to be previewed by *Variety*.

*Falconhead* (Michael Zen, 1977)—a movie featuring quintessential 1970s fashion such as fur rugs, chest hair, and a thick mustache—blended sex and artistic expression, and inspired several contemporary porn directors. It was also featured in a 2005 issue of *Unzipped Magazine*'s "100 Greatest Gay Adult Films Ever Made." *La Dolce Vita* (Michael Lucas, 2006) is known for being the most expensive gay porn film ever made, with its budget of $250,000. Although not in the film genre, Tom of Finland's homoerotic fetish art, with its infamously exaggerated physical features, is considered among the most influential imagery in gay pornography.

More recent to the scene, queer porn has begun pushing the boundaries of gender and sexuality without recreating the stereotypes so often found in mainstream porn. Jiz Lee, Courtney Trouble, Cinnamon Maxxine, Papí Coxxx, James Darling, and Shine Louise Houston are among the many notable performers and producers working in the genre.

# 3

# THE PORNOGRAPHY INDUSTRY

Although pornography has existed for centuries, the pornography *industry* has not. As described in the previous chapter about the history of pornography, development of the porn industry has gone hand in hand with changes in technology and economics. Shifting moral concerns and legal decisions have also impacted the business of creating, distributing, and consuming porn. Regulations define how legal porn is produced, with on-the-books production in Los Angeles requiring permits and STI (sexually transmitted infection) testing. Production and distribution of legal pornography is intended to be transparent, but the case is that business practices are neither always legal nor transparent. The above-board companies and trade organizations are well known, and some porn-related corporations are publicly traded. The financial side of the business, however, is often shrouded by secrecy, misinformation, and even piracy.

### What Is the Difference between Mainstream and Indie Porn?

Mainstream and independent (indie) porn are distinguished on the basis of two general features: (a) how the content is made and distributed and (b) what kind of content is featured.

The business model for independent porn differs from mainstream porn in that an effort is made to create equitable and ethical financial agreements. That's not to say that mainstream porn is always unethical or that indie porn always is. However, it is far more likely to find independent, queer, and feminist pornographers with a stated commitment to producing fair trade, ethical content.

Some indie companies, for example, pay a flat rate regardless of gender, experience, or what is done on camera. Pink and White Productions has equal pay for performers through projects such as CrashPadSeries.com or HeavenlySpire.com (director Shine Louise Houston's masculine appreciation site). With Pink and White's work, the performers are able to have whatever kind of sex they want with some parameters such as no feces, menses, and so forth. Crash Pad has performers who are ciswomen, transwomen, transmen, and occasionally cismen, as well as genderqueer performers. (The term *cis* means that gender identity and the sex one is assigned at birth are in alignment.) Indie porn actor Jiz Lee explains that one flat rate—regardless of gender—keeps things fair and encourages performers' agency in choosing the sex act they feel the most comfortable and safest performing. Talent is only asked to do things they would like to do with their scene partners. The flat fee system means there is no pressure to do more for more money. It is unlikely that this model will be adapted by the mainstream industry at large, Lee speculates, but it is the standard practice used by independent and queer-focused production houses.

Ned Henry describes the blend of a progressive business model and content that defines indie porn and that he implemented with his partner when they built their brand, Meet the Mayhems. "We wanted a way to monetize our content on our own terms with little to no startup capital. To make this possible, we had to do everything ourselves, from programming and web development to videography, editing, legal issues, and publicity. This work gave us the freedom to present masculinity and femininity in new ways, to show hot sex acts we always wanted to see in porn and rarely did, and to find our own audience and create our own market."[1]

Innovative ventures, such as Pink and White Productions and Make Love Not Porn, aim to create porn alternatives that are distinguished from the mainstream in both its content and its business model. Former advertising executive Cindy Gallop describes MakeLoveNotPorn.tv as a radically disruptive website that features real-world sex. The business plan involves everyday people (the MakeLoveNotPornStars) uploading videos of themselves having sex. After these videos are curated, website subscribers can rent the videos for three weeks at $5.00 each. The profits are shared equally among the team running the site and the MakeLoveNotPornStars. Gallop's goal is "to provide an alternative to mainstream porn and to open up the conversation about sex in our culture, while developing a self-sustaining economy that rewards everyone involved."[2]

The problem is that banking industry policies and crowd-funding protocols aren't always on board with this sort of vision. Financial constraints can present serious challenges that impede new startups such as Gallop's, including those with progressive business models, egalitarian politics, and an appreciation for diverse sexual aesthetics. Investors are cautious, and small-business loans for porn startups are virtually impossible to get due to "morality clauses" in the banking industry. Many online crowd funding platforms, such as Kickstarter, don't officially allow porn-based projects to raise funding on their sites. Porn-friendly crowdfunding sites such as Offbeatr take 30 percent from fully funded projects. It is not unusual for banks to close down adult industry accounts, which interferes with business in innumerable ways. Furthermore, selling porn requires the ability to process credit cards. Payment services such as Amazon Payments, Google Wallet, and PayPal don't allow users to buy adult products. Visa and MasterCard, the two largest credit card companies, both consider "adult merchants" to be high risk. Their fees therefore include $500 to register with each network, and another $500 charged to each company, every year. Then there are the fees for processing credit card payments and the percentage of sales that the credit card companies and processors take off the top—that is, *if* the porn company can find a processor willing to work with them. For a business that often has a small profit margin, these costs and banking policies are prohibitive. What's more, Chase Bank has been known to shut down porn performers' personal bank accounts for no reason.

Despite the financial challenges for would-be independent pornographers, mainstream corporate porn catering to heterosexual (and often white) consumers has also taken a hit. DIY competition, pirating, technological changes moving access away from print and cable, and the 2008 Great Recession have all impacted the bottom line. But interestingly, not all genres of porn are suffering a similar decline. Because of technology, anyone with a cell phone can now make and distribute porn and thereby control the means of production—wresting monopoly control from large corporations, at least in some small way. Author and film director Tristan Taormino reports that "niche porn" is doing really well. Lesbian-produced lesbian porn, content produced by and for queer folks, and pornography made by and for trans people are doing really well, Taormino explains, because this material offers a really unique product to an underserved and underrepresented minority. There's a real market for this, says Taormino. It can be a refreshing alternative to the humdrum tropes of mainstream porn.

Author Jaclyn Friedman describes the generic choreography of mainstream heterosexual porn: the video ends when the man ejaculates. Women are presumably on display for the male viewer's orgasm, and female pleasure is portrayed as existing in the service of male sexuality. Porn that doesn't feature putatively straight women, white people, cisgender performers, and heterosexual coupling is marginalized as taboo or fetish. This gives viewers the repeated impression, says Friedman, that male ejaculation is the purpose of sex. This trope centers male pleasure and sexual satisfaction, and generally relegates women to the role of pleasure providers. What's more, mainstream pornography is often racist and transphobic. Indie porn, feminist, and queer porn subverts this heteronormative white patriarchal paradigm with the intention of expanding access and acceptability of pleasure for a broader cross section of people and desires.

### What Is the Difference between Features, Gonzo, and Unscripted Porn?

Feature films involve scripts, plot lines, elaborate costumes, soundtracks, and set design. There has been a resurgence of porn features that parody popular TV shows or mainstream blockbuster films such as *Whore of the Rings* (a play on *Lord of the Rings*); *Twinklight* (a gay twinks vampire saga spoofing *Twilight*); *Edward Penishands* (based on *Edward Scissorhands*); *Batman in Robin*; and *Miami Spice*, a play on the 1990s prime-time police drama, *Miami Vice*.

In contrast, gonzo porn has no plot line. Gonzo lacks backdrops and fancy costumes (or usually any clothing at all) and therefore requires a minimal budget. Gonzo can involve high levels of violence, but "violent porn" is not the definition of gonzo. Rather, it is the erasure of the so-called fourth wall where there is no pretense of separation between the performers and the viewers.

Unscripted porn uses minimal guidelines or none at all. For instance, the sex featured in Shine Louise Houston's *Crash Pad Series* is not scripted, which makes videos somewhat like erotic documentary. But even her features are largely unscripted. "Even in the scripted films I don't script the sex," Shine Louise Houston commented during a Reddit "Ask Me Anything" held on June 17, 2015. The sex is left up to the talent. "I shoot the narrative bits of the scene first then let them do what they want. In some scenes I ask that this person cum first or that they end up in this position in the end but mostly I don't direct the talent. I direct the cameras. For pros that can be intimidating but I find that I get great scenes when I'm not telling people what to do."

Hentai is Japanese cartoon pornography that is usually drawn in an exaggerated style. Hentai often features taboo themes such as tentacle porn in which creatures such as octopuses or aliens engage in often-unwilling sex acts with women; shotacon, which involves young boys; and incest or urination. Although hentai involves drawings, not actual people, it is often considered controversial and offensive because the characters are frequently based on children. Representation of minors is more common in hentai based on characters from well-known anime shows or manga series. The use of taboo in porn is certainly not unique to this genre.

### What Are Some of the Leading Industry Organizations and Publications?

Like any major industry, the pornography business is underscored by various organizations and professional publications. Examples of leading international adult trade shows include Venus Berlin, the largest international erotic fair, and Australia's AdultEx, the Southern Hemisphere's largest annual event featuring adult industry manufacturers and retailers.

Among the leading US-based industry organizations are *Xbiz* and *Adult Video News* (AVN). *Xbiz* is a global industry news source offering movie reviews, op-eds, legal news, and other information relevant to the adult industry. *AVN*, an industry trade journal, provides promotional information about video releases, porn performers, and entertainment activities. *AVN* also culls the news about research, legislation, and healthcare issues related to the adult industry and makes this information available through its website.

The Association of Sites Advocating Child Protection (ASACP) was founded in 1996 to battle child pornography. ASACP uses anonymous reporting mechanisms and education to reach parents, the online adult entertainment industry, international government policymakers, and the public about online child safety. ASACP efforts work cooperatively with the adult industry and stem from mutual concern about eradicating child sexual abuse and proactively addressing Internet child safety issues. Corporate sponsors include Girlfriend Films, Adult FriendFinder, and Saboom Interactive Porn, among many others.

The Licensed Adult Talent Agency Trade Association (LATATA) is a California-based organization intended to advance legally licensed and bonded talent agencies and the interest of their clients. This work is done through advocacy, education, and by promoting ethical trade practices. LATATA was formed to foster coalition-building between all licensed talent agencies for the adult entertainment business. Its primary goal is to promote the longevity and well-being of the adult entertainment industry. The Adult Performer Advocacy Committee (APAC) was established to represent adult performers and to protect their right to a safer and more professional work environment through education, developing ethical best practices, and by fostering solidarity. The Free Speech Coalition (FSC) is a national trade association for the adult entertainment industry and pleasure products. The FSC opposes all obscenity and censorship legislation (with the exception of laws that target piracy). In addition to lobbying and providing training seminars, the FSC offers member benefits including access to the First Entertainment Credit Union, insurance services, and record-keeping software that helps organize data to meet legal requirements for the adult industry.

### What Kind of Records Need to Be Kept?

Federal law requires primary and secondary producers of sexually explicit material to maintain impeccable records on all models for every production. The Child Protection and Obscenity Enforcement Act of 1988 is commonly referred to as the "2257 Regulations" or simply 2257. This federal law is intended to prevent child abuse and child exploitation. It requires proof that all models, actors, and other persons appearing in any visual depiction of actual sexually explicit conduct contained on adult websites (or other format) were over the age of eighteen years at the time such depictions were created. Other records on file include W-9s, release forms, legal disclaimers, photographs required by federal legislation, and proof of STI testing.

As for labor contracts, a few top performers are under contract with major studios such as Vivid Entertainment, Wicked Pictures, or Zero Tolerance. Exclusive contracts with major companies require that the talent maintain a positive image of an adult studio, appear in a specific number of movies, and promote the company at store signings, conventions, expos, and other events. In exchange, these performers are paid a regular salary. For the most part, though, porn actors are independent contractors. Far more common are "amateurs" who are trying to independently launch into the business or have a bit of fun. Others who are entirely trafficked or exploited do not have contracts and, in the cases of revenge porn and other crimes, may not even realize their images have been used in pornographic contexts.

### What Happens on a Porn Shoot?

Writing for SWAAY—Sex Work Activists, Allies, and You—performer Danny Wylde described what happens on a legal porn shoot. Once the paperwork is filled out and STI test results are shared, performers move on to the sex scene. Many productions take still photographs of each sexual position prior to shooting video to help streamline the plans for appropriate lighting. Some productions require "setups," or acting pieces, that build up to the sex scenes. These can be a few minutes long or they can take several hours to film, depending on the script and other variables on set. Adult performers' workdays last anywhere from two to twelve hours and even longer. Because no unions currently exist in the adult industry, working hours are not regulated.

If there is a man in the sex scene (which can last from twenty to forty minutes, if all goes as planned), the male performer ejaculates somewhere on the female's body or face, or on another man in gay productions. Due to the pressure put on the male to ejaculate on cue, the end of sex scenes are often prearranged. This allows ample time for the male performer to masturbate until he is ready to climax. Once he is about to ejaculate, he alerts the video crew and the moment is filmed. After the sex scene is finished, the performers are given baby wipes and paper towels, and usually have the option to take a shower.[3]

Kevin Moore, who produces films for Evil Angel, describes the process similarly, adding details about pre- and postproduction. The actual scenes are about 50 percent of the entire process. A lot of the work before and after the main scene is unsexy and boring, Moore says. It involves details such as planning what and who to shoot, securing locations, editing, and handling paperwork. "Every day I get ten to twenty emails from new girls, or from women who are new to L.A. or who will be in town while they're traveling. I go through those and see if there's someone I want to shoot in upcoming videos." In large companies such as Brazzers (which is owned by Mindgeek), the company typically decides whom to hire. But Evil Angel follows a unique business model by which the producer retains control of the product and therefore retains independent control over hiring cast and crew. Still, many of the protocols and procedures follow a similar pattern across the industry.

Booking talent is a combination of culling the data, working with agents, and a gut-level feeling about the performer. There are more booking agents than ever before who are working with female talent, Moore comments. Freeones.com provides clips and data about female performers and charts who's popular. The site's Top Ten is an important casting resource because this list is driven by traffic. Analytics from social media provide another source of data about a woman's popularity, who's on the rise or decline, and what kind of porn is trending. (Moore explains, for instance, that in 2015, pseudo-incest porn was a popular genre.)

There is no real data for the guys in porn. Casting men, however, is a bit different, Moore explains. A woman can be beautiful but a mediocre performer—and still be successful in porn. A mediocre guy, however, doesn't work well for this line of work. There are lots of men in the industry, but they probably face the highest bars for performance in the business, says Moore. It's the difference between an excellent athlete and an "okay" athlete. There is a lot of demand for excellent male talent in pornography and not that many of the good ones.

On the day of a shoot, call times are early. After makeup and wardrobe is finished, solo still photos are taken. These photos are called "Pretty Girls," and they take a fair amount of time. The video scenes are highly fantasy driven and, Moore admits, are purely designed to appeal to heterosexual men. Most scenes are not highly scripted; as the director, Moore lays the general groundwork for the shoot and establishes the fantasy and the look of the shoot. "After that, it is up to the talent to dance," says Moore. "I step in if movements are weird or if there's not enough interaction with the camera. I like things prettier than some of the Evil Angel productions, but I still like good sex in my shoots . . . I break down the fourth wall in my videos, which means the talent seems to be engaging with the viewer. I try to avoid stopping, or cutting, scenes because that destroys the flow and it takes a toll on the talent." That said, breaks are frequent, and performers can always stop a scene if they are uncomfortable. Porn sex doesn't happen in someone's own bed and it's a performance for the camera, Moore continues. Sometimes people have to hold awkward positions for a fair amount of time, or they're having sex on a hard desk or something. Talent can always say, "Hey, this hurts," or "I'm uncomfortable." Then we stop shooting the scene and readjust the positions so that it's easier on the performer. "This happens a lot," Moore says. Shooting porn "is not a party. It really isn't. Everyone works hard—the performers, the crew, every-one. The professional companies look at the work in a professional way, even though this industry is looked down on. If a person spent two weeks on a set, they would come away with a very different idea about what working in pornography is really like."

Somewhat different from the semiscripted features that Moore produces, The Crash Pad Series involves a clandestine San Francisco apartment where a voyeuristic landlord supplies keys to the pleasure-seeking visitors so that she can watch their sexual escapades through hidden cameras. Director Shine Louise Houston describes an average "day-in-the-life" on the set of a Crash Pad porn shoot:

> I set out snacks and coffee, and prep the cameras. Around ten am the cast and crew arrive. We go over paper work, take ID photos, and then talent takes their profile pics for the website. The profile photos can be clothed or nude depending on what they're comfortable with, and talent can do their scene in whatever state of undress they choose. We've had some folks do their scene fully clothed. Then the models usually check in with each other about do's and don'ts. Right before we shoot I go over the fun stuff where I ask them what they'd like to do today. They'll let me know if the scene is going to incorporate BDSM [Bondage and Discipline; Sadism and Masochism; Dominance and Submission] or toys or where they'd like to start in the studio: on the couch, in the living room, etc. So once we've loosely mapped out where and what they want to do we head to set. I usually turn on the live cam at this point.
>
> Our live cam is a bit different than most. We don't play to the camera, it's just a fly on the wall. Site members get to see how the magic happens. After the scene, talent will take a break, we clean up set, and get ready for the post-sex interview. In the post-sex interview, I ask what

they liked about the scene, what was challenging, what their safe-sex practices are and why, and why they keep doing porn. I love this part of the day. Then everyone in invited to lunch before we do it all over again for the second shoot of the day.

As for equipment, it is entirely possible to shoot porn using a cell phone and upload it with a fast Internet connection. The days of needing expensive gear, and film and photo developing skills to produce porn are in the past. However, established companies use high-end gear. Pink and White Productions employs various cameras and lenses such as the Panasonic AF100 with C-Mount cine lenses, a combination of Kino and Tungsten lightbulbs, 250-watt spotlights, and "practicals" scattered around the set, meaning lights that can be controlled by the talent and sometimes altered for brightness or color.

### How Much Does It Cost to Produce Porn?

The cost of production can vary widely depending on the type of pornography, the budget, location, and the amount of available funding. In addition to hiring sex-worker talent, porn production employs service workers and technical teams—food caterers, makeup artists, security personnel, accountants, attorneys, publicists, and behind-the-scenes workers.

Although pornography is made around the world, the San Fernando Valley is the place best known for legal (and illegal) porn production. Most American porn is made in California because the State Supreme Court decided in 1988 that getting paid to have sex on camera is legally protected speech and not prostitution. Yet pornography is produced around the country despite the fact that no other state has made a similar a ruling.

In part due to the cost impact of Measure B, which now mandates condom use for all porn made in Los Angeles County, there is chatter among industry insiders that film shoots may be increasingly moving to Florida, Brazil, Eastern Europe, and Las Vegas. The number of permits requested to make porn films in Los Angeles County has declined by an estimated 95 percent since the law took effect. According to FilmL.A., the number of film permit applications fell from about 480 in 2012 to just 40 in 2013, and only 36 in 2014. By July 2015, only 7 permits had been issued for the year. Whereas Los Angeles charges hundreds of dollars for location permits, Clark County, Nevada, only charges a nominal fee (and does not require condoms). Las Vegas offers other financial incentives as well. The state of Nevada does not charge corporate income tax, and the cost of living in Las Vegas is more affordable than Los Angeles. Still, the legality of filming porn in Las Vegas and the feasibility of moving an entire industry remains to be seen. Moreover, the figures showing a declining number of film permits pulled in Los Angeles does not necessarily prove there are fewer adult productions as a result of Measure B; this may instead reflect an increasing number of unpermitted shoots.

Regardless, however, of where porn shoots are located and whether they're legally permitted, there is little high-end production in the mainstream industry these days says Adam Grayson, Chief Financial Officer for Evil Angel. Of current productions, 95 percent are gonzo shoots. This means there is minimal crew, lower production value, and therefore lower production cost. A few select companies such as Wicked still use more elaborate production setups, but this is unusual given changes in technology, the industry, and the broader economy.

An average porn shoot in Los Angeles includes the director, a production assistant, makeup artists, and crew. The director is often also the one holding the camera. General parameters hold true for both mainstream and indie shoots, depending on the scope of the production. The pay rates are generally $150 per scene for each crew member; makeup artists earn between $100 and $150 per person, and often work on several shoots during the course of a day. Grayson points out that professionally done makeup is even more important these days given the use of photo stills and the need for images to really pop on camera and online.

Other line item costs may include food, wardrobe, baby wipes, and sex toys. Given that most are not large-scale productions but cost-effective shoots, these amounts are minimal. Insurance premiums and film permit costs are additional production costs. However, as Grayson explains, the director usually absorbs these costs at a range of $3,000 to $4,000 a year. Wicked is one company that fully insures its shoots, but many productions simply fall short of that. As mentioned, because of changes in the law that now require condom use in Los Angeles County, permits are often not pulled for shoots and, for the most part, permits are not enforced.

The cost for locations varies but is relatively modest. Again, it is rare these days for porn productions to use a fully constructed set. More commonly, porn shoots take place in private homes. Even though gonzo shoots have relatively low budgets, location is one cost where gonzo is spending more than it used to. "A junky place in Canoga Park can run $200 for the entire shoot," says Grayson. Nice houses—with no structures impeding the view and a hilltop location that provides maximum natural light—are preferred by directors. This will cost about $100 an hour and can run from $800 to $1,000 for the day.

Tristan Taormino comments that rates vary wildly depending on the company you work for. In general terms, she says, daily production costs break down as follows: camera operators earn $500 to $700, grip and lighting equipment rental costs between $600 and $800, sound engineers earn between $200 and $400, and the best boy (lighting) is paid $350.

Production managers and still photographers all earn about $500 a day, with production earning far less at $150 to $250 a day. Directors earn either a flat rate or they receive a budget from the studio and get to keep whatever they don't spend on production, crew, talent, locations, and editing. This amount can range from nothing to about $5,000, Taormino says.

Adam Grayson echoes this latter point. The business model used by Evil Angel involves hiring directors to produce pornography while Evil Angel takes care of distribution. This means directors finance their own movies, pay for any permits and insurance, and assume all responsibility for the shoot. Unless money is advanced to the director (which could then be legally perceived as a joint venture), should anything go wrong, the distribution company can claim plausible deniability. Evil Angel only charges a distribution fee, which means the director owns the film in perpetuity and, depending on their financing and budgeting skills, can earn their profit accordingly.

### How Much Revenue Does Pornography Generate . . . and How Accurate Are These Figures?

Information about porn revenue is notoriously difficult to ascertain. One often-repeated figure is that people spend $3,000 every second on Internet porn; another is that industry revenues surpass earnings by Microsoft, Google, Amazon, eBay, Yahoo, Apple, and Netflix combined. Although dramatic, this comparison is untrue. Among the reasons for miscalculations and skewed statements about the financial aspects of the adult industry is the fact that multiple revenue streams fall under the pornography umbrella, there are countless online content providers, and sometimes-sloppy record-keeping.

"Porn is all over the Internet, but the actual size of the industry is a mystery," writes Stephanie Pappas for *Live Science*. "No one keeps official records, and few studies have made a stab at the economics of porn."[4] *Adult Video News* can only estimate the amount of porn sales and rentals. Accordingly, *AVN* senior editor Mark Kernes claimed in 2007 that retail sales reached $6 billion a year. *AVN*'s figures are widely disputed; yet in January 2015, CNBC reported that the adult entertainment business is a $14 billion-a-year industry—more than twice the disputed figures from years prior. Melissa Harris-Perry reported on a

2015 episode of her MSNBC news show that revenue from the porn industry is between $5 and $12 billion.

When it comes to cable and satellite television revenue, adult content has, in the past, been a consistent source of profit. According to analysts, cable operators have the leverage to command margins that have exceeded 90 percent on rentals of generally interchangeable porn movies. In 2008, pay-per-view and adult video-on-demand peaked with earnings of $1 billion. However, the revenue earned by cable, satellite, and telecommunications companies providing this service dropped to about $899 million in 2010. Following a similar pattern, domestic TV revenue by Playboy Enterprises Inc., for example, reached $75.8 million in 2007 before falling to $44.4 million in 2010 as a result of DIY porn production, pirating, and consumer migration from television to online content. Friendfinder, Inc., a publicly traded porn company that owns the Penthouse brand, mirrors the patterns for other, similar companies: Friendfinder's revenue declined from $346 million in 2010 to $331 million by 2011. (That same year, CEO and Director Mark H. Bell earned a salary topping $800,000.)

Across the industry, overall, Diane Duke, CEO of the FSC estimated that revenue dropped by 50 percent between 2007 and 2012. Yet beyond the reported revenue data based on securities filing, *The Wall Street Journal* explains it is often "hard to get a fix on how much porn contributes to companies' bottom lines" because not all companies are transparent about their earnings.[5]

In researching an article on pornography for Atlantic Media Company's online news outlet, *Quartz*, journalist and former *Hustler* editor Lee Quarnstrom faced the challenge of finding reliable revenue figures. "The editors [at *Quartz*] were completely freaked out by the lack of specificity of numerical things—such as how many people visit porn websites every day or month. So they did their own research to come up with enough numbers to ease their editorial fears," Quarnstrom comments.[6] Even vocal anti-porn activist Gail Dines, who reports in her book *Pornland* that the global porn industry was worth about $96 billion in 2006, notes, "finding reliable data on the industry is almost impossible so you have to assume that the statistics are approximate at best. The most quoted stats come from Internet Filter," Dines says. "But," she cautions, "I am not sure how accurate they are."[7] What isn't contested is that *Hustler*'s monthly circulation dropped from a high of 3 million readers in the 1970s to a mere 100,000 in 2014, a shift so dramatic that Larry Flynt doesn't expect *Hustler* to last beyond 2017. *Playboy* announced in 2015 that the magazine would no longer print nude photos of women given the impact of online pornography.

It is difficult to deduce revenue from page views. But, in terms of online traffic, Pornhub is arguably the most frequently visited online porn site, with 78 billion page views in 2014 alone. Pornhub's global Alexa ranking—a system that audits the frequency of traffic to various websites—is higher than CNN, BuzzFeed, and Huffington Post. The company claims that it uses algorithms to create a highly curated, personalized site based on a user's keyword search history, location, and even the time of day they log on. Another way of looking at this business model is that it spoon-feeds a limited range of content to unsuspecting online porn users who do not realize their online porn-use patterns are largely molded by a large corporation. Like other media conglomerates, Pornhub's business model features vertical integration (e.g., content partners Brazzers, Mofos, Digital Playground, and Twistys) and, increasingly, horizontal integration as well. Pornhub is owned by MindGeek, which owns a network of additional distribution sites such as Xtube and YouPorn. Pornhub's reach extends beyond the pornography business to a recently launched record label and its analytics blog. Because Pornhub is a network of highly accessed URL tube sites (meaning they collect and steer traffic to illegal downloads), many adult performers believe that Pornhub directly contributes to the adult industry's economic decline.

### Stolen Porn: What Is Internet Piracy?

Online piracy impacts all sectors of content creation from music to movies. By some reports, it is estimated that stolen porn impacts the adult industry by about $2 billion per year. One factor that exacerbates the problem is that in the current Internet climate, porn users often don't think using free porn is criminal or unethical. The fact is that stolen porn violates copyright law and is a rampant problem faced by the adult industry. Pirated—or stolen—porn includes a variety of formats such as bootlegged copies of content, unauthorized DVD sales, illegal screen grabs, torrent files, and tube sites.

Bootlegged content involves copies of pornography that are made without copyright permission. Unauthorized resellers are websites that sell these illegal copies of movies, videos, DVDs, or photo images. Torrent sites enable the illegal sharing of large data files. These are peer-to-peer sites where users trade copyrighted content directly among themselves. Tube sites post pirated streaming video online for user access.

Some illegal product resellers use mainstream auction sites such as eBay to sell their stolen content; others establish sites that are specifically established for the illegal sale and transfer of pornography. According to Takedown Piracy, these sites are often set up in Hong Kong because they are harder to reach through litigation. Mainstream social media is increasingly used to announce the release of newly stolen material: blogs, specialized search engines, and even Twitter are used for content announcements. Once the announcements are made, cyberlockers—online storage sites that are not searchable—can be used as a repository for pirated porn.

### What Efforts Are Being Made to Address Porn Piracy?

The adult industry has made several moves to combat porn piracy including massive lawsuits, threats of public exposure, and digital fingerprinting technology that helps track down stolen porn. Companies such as Evil Angel and Girlfriend

Films have each employed a full-time person tasked with finding pirated films and clips online and making sure they are taken off the Internet. One common practice is to send Digital Millennium Copyright Act (DMCA) notices to the offending parties, thus putting them on notice that they have violated the law. In 2014, a social media campaign was launched under the hashtag #PayForYourPorn in an effort by performers to hold their fans accountable and encourage them to buy the porn they use.

Organizations such as Porn Guardian find and remove infringing links to adult content, sending DCMA notices at a rate of every fifteen minutes. Porn Guardian assists with legal support and digital fingerprinting and even contacts billing companies or advertisers to cut off funding to the offending sites, if necessary. Nate Glass owns the antipiracy organization, Takedown Piracy, which provides tracking and recourse for companies and performers concerned about porn theft. As of April 30, 2015, Takedown Piracy had removed more than 56 million online copyright infringements.

In an effort to find a solution to the problem of rampant pirating, some legitimate pornography companies have tried to partner with tube sites to split the revenue. Nate Glass disagrees with this strategy. "I've never believed in partnering with tube sites—it's a deal with the Devil," says Glass. "Too often copyright holders have tried to monetize piracy by searching for a middle ground with the tube sites. At the end of the day, the tube sites make more money from pirated content than trying to monetize a promotional trailer. Because of this, the tubes will never have enough incentive to totally clean up their act."[8] In this view, effective solutions require strong measures (e.g., lawsuits and digital fingerprinting) that remove infringing content from tube sites and search engines, such as Google, and return the power of controlling the content back to the content creator.

Speaking at the Adult Entertainment Expo, Glass commented that the porn industry's fight against tube sites (such

as Pornhub) is like the music and film industries fighting illegal music and movie downloads. In addition to legal battles,
the strategy for successfully circumventing digital theft has
been to create pay-for-use models such as iTunes, Netflix, and
other similar sites. The challenge, Glass notes, is that because
free porn has become so ubiquitous, successfully charging
customers for a monthly subscription could be a challenge.[9]

A newer strategy in combatting porn theft is to bring back
plot-driven porn. Writing for *Slate*, journalist Tracy Clark-Flory
explains the idea behind this approach. "If the sex scenes are
made sexy by the larger, complex narrative at hand—rather
than the shorthand of X-rated clichés, like the naughty school-
girl or the MILF next door—they won't end up as free jerk-off
material on Pornhub." The inaugural launch of this plan is a
long-form video titled *Marriage 2.0*. The movie features a novel
blend of well-known authors, educators, and porn performers
including Christopher Ryan, coauthor of the *New York Times*
bestseller *Sex at Dawn*; sexologist Carol Queen; sex educator
Reid Mihalko; and adult performers India Summer, Dylan
Ryan, and Nina Hartley. Studios such as Adam & Eve, Wicked,
New Sensations, and Girlfriends are getting on board with
this new strategy by also producing story-driven feature films
in which the sex scenes support the movie rather than serving
as stand-alone clips.

### What Are the Awards Given for Porn?

Much like the Oscars or the Golden Globes, the pornography
industry also provides awards for acclaimed performances.
The Adult Awards, working in tandem with Xbiz London,
features various categories for achievement and excellence in
the UK adult entertainment industry. In addition to awards for
talent in categories such as Best Male Model and Best Female
Mature Model, awards are also given for distribution and
behind the scenes production work. These categories include,
for example, Best Production Studio, Best Payment Service

Provider, and Best Graphic Design Studio. AVN hosts a similar annual award show in Las Vegas honoring the year's top adult actors and best movies. Compared with the AVN awards, those given by Xbiz tend to focus a bit more on the business side of the industry. Xbiz awards include a voting component for Xbiz staff and verified industry members. Xbiz also added online voting, in some categories, so that fans can weigh in.

The annual Grabby Awards—or simply, The Grabbys—is a Chicago-based event to honor work done in the gay adult video industry. The first awards were given in 1991 by a listing in the *Gay Chicago Magazine*; the first public awards ceremony was held in 1999 in conjunction with the annual International Mister Leather Contest. The Blatino Erotica Awards were launched to recognize the often-overlooked contributions of gay and bisexual men of African or Latino descent. The similarly named FlavaMen Blatino Awards also recognizes gay men of color in the adult industry.

The Feminist Porn Awards was first launched in 2006 to recognize and celebrate those who make quality films with high production value that do not rely on sexual stereotypes. These emerging films are directed in particular by people of color, trans folks, queers, and lesbians and feature their communities without being fetishized—and with respect. The first awards were called "The Emmas" in honor of the pro-sex anarchist feminist Emma Goldman (1869–1940) who rejected any control over women's bodies or sexuality. The Feminist Porn Awards chose a butt plug as the symbol of the award to represent sexuality (everyone has one), regardless of sex, gender, or orientation. In addition to the awards gala, The Feminist Porn Awards includes a separate screening night showcasing the diversity of the year's submissions. The annual event is held in Toronto. Other international porn awards include the Australian Adult Industry Awards and the Adult Broadcasting Awards in Japan.

# 4

# PORN PERFORMERS

## *How Much Are Porn Performers Paid?*

This is the question that people can mistakenly assume has a million-dollar answer. Adult entertainment is a global industry that employs up to 20,000 people in California's San Fernando Valley alone. In general, most performances garner between $200 and $1,200. The pay rate for adult performers can vary widely, though, depending on the contract, the hiring company, the kind of sex required, the actor's race and gender, and oftentimes the experience or notoriety of the performer, as negotiated. An annual porn performer's salary can also vary greatly based on how often they get booked to work. If a female performer shoots a two-person, heterosexual, anal sex scene three times a month, she could make a $40,000 annual salary. However, yearly estimates are nearly impossible to generalize because rates vary and the frequency of filming is impossible to predict. Payment is based on a flat rate per scene or photo shoot, regardless of whether the movie (or photo still) sells well or not. Moreover, as explained in chapter 3, widespread porn theft and the easy availability of free online porn greatly impacts porn performers' earnings.

A few well-known people like James Deen or Nina Hartley have become high-earning household names, but this is not the case for the vast majority of adult entertainers. Jenna Jameson's net worth is reportedly $10 million—earned from book royalties, producer's credits, directing, and entrepreneurship but not exclusively from her sex performance. Jameson is the exception, not the rule—and it is worth noting that few industry insiders will go on record with precise salary figures.

According to adult talent agent Mark Spiegler, who represents top female performers, the annual pay among the highest earners once reached $100,000 a year; today the pay is half as much and requires constant publicity through social media and personal appearances. According to Spiegler, in-demand actresses are paid according to a relatively straightforward scale. This includes $800 for lesbian scenes, $1,000 for heterosexual scenes, $1,200 or more for anal sex, and at least $4,000 for double penetration. There is reason to believe that Spiegler's account (and others like it) is overinflated. Writing for the *New Statesman*, well-known performer Stoya shares that pay is not openly discussed among porn actors. Whispers about pay rates and working conditions can include very inaccurate figures. For example, Stoya says, a famous performer from the 2000's claimed her rate for double penetration was $12,000. (Double penetration involves two men penetrating a woman's anus and vagina.) Stoya set her rates accordingly and was paid about half that amount after negotiations. Stoya later found out the original actress had far overstated her pay. The actual amount she received for double penetration scenes was $1,200 to $1,400. In this case, another performer's financial lie happened to work in Stoya's favor. More often, though, "the lack of transparency regarding pay leads to newer performers undervaluing themselves and their work." The solution is to "drag the numbers into the sunshine and to discuss them openly," Stoya says. Putting her money where her mouth is, Stoya went on public record with how much she paid the ten performers in the film she funded and directed called *Graphic Depictions*: each performer with a penis (her words) was paid an average of $750 per scene for a total of $4,500 allotted to pay male performers; $1,050 went to performers with vulvas, three of whom identify as female and one who is gender-neutral, for a total of $4,200. One performer was hired through an agency, requiring an additional $100 fee for booking. The cost to the performer for appearing in a movie includes transportation to the set—sometimes from a different city, or even state or country—an "insane level of personal grooming"; and STI testing, which by Stoya's calculations costs between $155 and $210.[1]

Industry magazine *Xbiz* reports that there are about 250 "in-demand" female performers who shoot between 100 and 150 scenes per year. But, for most, the frequency of work is far less. What's more, the average length of a porn performer's career is a short one, lasting four to six months.

### How Do Rates Vary?

The rates for video porn scenes vary based on the performer's gender and the kind of sex performed. Scenes involving high-risk sex, such as anal creampies (internal ejaculate that is squeezed out), pay the most; those with no genital penetration generally pay less. There can be an exception when it comes to fetish work. Porn pay in the United States is the highest compared to Germany, Canada, Australia, and the United Kingdom. Frequently, people of color and fat performers report lower compensation. Because there is no regulated rate, pay can vary from performer to performer and from company to company.

Although men are hired more frequently than women, the adult industry is the only field where women consistently earn more. On average, men earn between $200 and $600 per scene doing straight porn, depending on their build and penis size. More specifically, male tops for a B/G (boy/girl) shoot earn far less at $200 to $400, but the pay jumps to between $400 and $500 if they bottom anally for transwomen or ciswomen. Some men are paid a mere $50 if the scene only includes receiving a heterosexual blow job and the performer "completes" the scene. Again, however, the rates vary depending on the type of scene (e.g., barebacking, group scenes, etc.), the location (i.e., permitted shoots within Los Angeles County, outside of L.A., etc.), and the producer's budget. Zero Tolerance Entertainment only pays amateur male performers $100 to $200 per scene, although director and award winner Courtney Cummz explains, "very few performers will openly discuss accepting low rates. Everyone wants to be seen as on top."[2]

Big-name gay male porn stars can earn up to $5,000 a scene, but the scale for gay male porn generally ranges from $500 to $1,000 per scene, and many performers only film about five scenes a month. Gay-for-pay performers—men who are heterosexual in their personal lives and perform gay sex for the porn industry—earn the same as gay performers. Some industry insiders and fans object to gay-for-pay performers, arguing that this takes work away from gay men. "Crossovers," meaning gay men who do straight porn, often find that female performers will refuse to work with them due to fears about STI and HIV risk, despite rigorous testing and condom use. This obviously impacts earnings potential.

A female model makes about $300 to $500 for a solo shoot. If the scene involves BDSM (Bondage and Discipline; Sadism and Masochism; Dominance and Submission) or if anal toys are involved, women earn between $500 and $600. If a female is with another female, the range is $500 to $900. If she is with a male performer, the pay ranges from $600 to $1,400. This rate depends on whether she is being penetrated vaginally or orally; and if the scene includes kink, creampie, internal cumshots, and so forth. As with male performers, oral-only shoots, such as blow-job scenes, can pay a lot less. Racism within the industry also impacts pay rates. Porn scholar Mireille Miller-Young has documented the pay disparity in the United States, where black women earn between 50 and 75 percent of what white women earn for a hard-core film. In countries such as Brazil or Hungary, where wages are depressed and the average minimum wage is very low, the pay scale for acting in porn is relatively quite high. Another way of looking at this is to understand that porn produced in poor countries is linked to intense exploitation of the workers.

A transwoman can make about the same as a ciswoman performer if she tops (to completion) in a shoot. The rate is about the same for a penetration scene between a cisfemale performer and transwoman performer as it is for a ciswoman and cisman. There is no industry standard where transmen are concerned.

### What Is the Pay for Magazine Shoots and Adult-Themed Products?

In the late 1970s, when glossy magazines were a more common form of pornography, *Hustler* paid female models a few hundred dollars for three- and four-page "girl sets." They earned an extra $500 if chosen to be on the cover. In total, women earned up to $1,500 if they were on the cover and also in a several-page spread inside the magazine. By the mid-1990s, *Playboy* was paying its centerfold models $25,000—with $20,000 for the print layout and $5,000 for the video portion. This amount remains the same in 2015. (For its editorial content, *Playboy* is known to pay relatively unknown writers up to $8,500 for 6,000-word articles.)

Playmates have additional income opportunities through personal appearances and thematic editorials, which usually involve several women posing as airline flight attendants, musicians, or some other motif scene. The pay for these layouts is $1,500. Personal appearances at casinos and other venues pay $500 for four hours and $1,500 for an eight-hour day. The requirements include wearing revealing outfits and meet-and-greets with fans. In the words of one Playboy bunny, there is no sex or nudity, just the expectation of congeniality, fun, and goodwill. An off-the-record model shares that playmates wear revealing outfits of their choice for these personal appearances; if they choose to wear the Playboy bunny costume, they are paid an extra $100 a day because the design and fit is so uncomfortable. Today, however, the opportunity for playmates to earn additional income at live events is limited. Requests for appearances have gone virtual, with fans requesting (and receiving) free photos posted to Instagram and other social media.

Porn-related retail products such as Fleshlights or dildos provide additional financial opportunity for some adult stars. John Holmes, Shane Diesel, and Jessica Drake are among those with eponymous products based on body molds made from their genitals. The cost for these sex toys runs between $80 and $90 at retail stores. In 2009, April Flores's vaginal anatomy was featured as the first CyberSkin Voluptuous Pussy mold made from a "Big Beautiful Woman" (BBW) retailing for $169.95.

For proprietary and privacy reasons, the percentage of profit that goes to the adult performers behind the products is difficult data to come by. Many industry insiders are unwilling to go on record with information about dollars and cents. Fleshlight, however, has a reputation for being one of the best royalty-based products for performers to engage their fans.

Some performers supplement their income by cultivating their fan base and then bartering for items through online Wish Lists by exchanging promo stills or signed DVDs. For example, Courtney Trouble (director of *BFF Pussy*) launched a crowdfunding venture to pay for graduate school and maintains an Amazon Wish List that is tweeted out to fans. Items include everyday needs and luxury goods ranging from vamp-colored lipstick and peep-toe pumps, to a pink KitchenAid professional food mixer with matching bowls. Trouble, of course, is just one example of the many others who maintain Wish Lists using their professional names.

Although not frequently utilized in the industry by performers, Affiliate Programs replace a royalties-based business model where performers can link to work that they've done with various studios through a code that tracks sale transactions. The financial yield for performers is 30 to 60 percent commission.

In sum, roughly 20 to 30 percent of performers' income is generated by activities outside porn videos, including stripping, personalized sex-toy designs, and paid website subscriptions. Although it veers into illegal activity and is not openly discussed, some porn performers supplement their incomes by also doing paid escort work. Other performers intentionally develop a presence in porn to bolster their escorting career. Women who have made a name for themselves through porn can charge up to $1,500 an hour for private escorting. These rates are potentially far more lucrative than the per-scene rate of pay currently offered in the Los Angeles-based industry.

When it comes to legal crossover work, there are opportunities in mainstream business ventures that are sometimes available for the most well-known performers. James Deen's branded clothing line is distributed through Girlfriend Films; *The Hollywood Reporter* notes Sunny Leone's Bollywood fame, Ron Jeremy's eponymous rum, Asa Akira's appearance in a G-Unit music video, and Sasha Grey's role in the HBO show *Entourage*. Michelle Sinclair's (Belladonna) appearance in Paul Thomas Anderson's film *Inherent Vice* is another example of mainstream crossover. But these opportunities are rare.

### What Are Cam Sites and How Much Do Performers Earn?

Live webcam shows, or cam sites, involve running a webcam, chatting with customers online, performing a variety of on-camera sex acts (usually solo), and going into private "rooms" when customers decide to pay for the performer's time. Once a private session starts, the customer pays by the minute to keep the live video streaming. Cam work is basically a live sex show made possible through Internet technology. The majority of cam performers are female. The audience demand for cam work is primarily male. Most cam sites cater to heterosexual men; others are geared toward a gay male audience. To date, there is limited cam work marketed toward women and queer identified people, although this could certainly change.

Among the most popular cam sites is LiveJasmin, which logs about 30 million visitors every month.

Proto cam work (1979–1992) blurred the lines between pornography and performance, starting with "talk-and-type" chat rooms. With changes in technology, photos could be downloaded; and soon modem, cable, and then Wi-Fi connections encouraged a camming boom.

Like many in the business, BBW performer Betty Blac does both video porn and cam work. In an interview with Mireille Miller-Young for *New Views on Pornography*, Blac explained that when she cams, customers have the option of tipping in the public room or taking her private. Customers pay $5.99 a minute, and she receives 40 percent of any money made. Some of the major companies stream cam sessions and get 20 or 30 percent. There are smaller, more feminist, companies, such as Skin Video, where "cam girls" make 80 percent; but they don't have the traffic volume of more well-known companies such as Kink.com or Streamit.com. Like all forms of the entertainment business, income varies dramatically. For US-based performers like Betty Blac, some nights might net merely $10, whereas a good night can range from $300 to $1,000. According to *Forbes*, however, nearly all of the webcam girls are from Eastern Europe or Southeast Asia, earning $8 to $15 an hour with no benefits.

### What Is It Like to Work in Porn?

Every job has its challenges, but because pornography involves intimate body parts and performing in public what are generally private acts, the on-the-job challenges can be unique.

One common question is about men's erections and how they can last so long. According to porn lore, a fluffer's role is to keep male performers erect. A bit of informal assistance may be used on set from time to time. But despite the fact that fluffers have been featured in movie themes and television plot lines, the job title is a myth say performers Aurora Snow and James Deen.

Since Viagra came on the market in 1998, men's erectile performance issues are less common than they use to be. Fetish porn producer Lance Hart explains that most of the men he works with try Viagra, Levitra, Cialis, or some sort of herbal product. There is also the erectile dysfunction medication TriMix-gel and its injectable version, which is administered directly into the penis. Both enable men to maintain erections for hours. However, no erectile product completely compensates for hunger or physical exhaustion that can happen during a long shoot.

Off-label use of erectile dysfunction medication among porn actors far exceeds the public average among young men. Actor Danny Wylde stopped working in front of the camera after an eight-year stint with Cialis and injectable Bimix left him at risk of serious medical harm. Faced with the possibility of never being able to achieve an erection again, Wylde retired from performing at the age of 28. (He now works behind the scenes.)

As Tracy Clark-Flory reports for *The Fix*, "ED drugs, especially injectables, are more out in the open on gay porn shoots, partly because of the constant flow of inexperienced male talent and so-called 'gay-for-pay' performers in need of assistance becoming aroused. 'On straight porn sets, guys try to hide it a little more because of machismo,' or because they think some women are uncomfortable knowing 'a guy has a medicated erection,'" says Danny Wylde.[3]

Maintaining an erection for hours is not the only on-the-job challenge that is unique to working in porn. Bondage scenes can also have distinctive challenges. Trussing can inhibit blood flow, and zip ties can cause itching. The sheer physicality of performing for the camera can require agility far beyond most everyday sex with possible risk of mechanical injury and repetitive strain. A misplaced stiletto heel can cause bruising and fire play can burn if poorly administered. Former porn performer Shelley Lubben claims that physical violence, name-calling, and drug use is not uncommon on porn sets. (Lubben, a high profile, born-again Christian, founded Pink Cross Foundation, a faith-based charity offering adult industry workers emotional, financial, and transitional support. Lubben has been accused of being an unreliable witness who is prone to lies and exaggeration.)

Anti-pornography activist Gail Dines has repeatedly claimed that anal sex scenes cause rampant rectal prolapse and that some women who are repeatedly penetrated by numerous men on porn shoots, often after taking handfuls of painkillers, require vaginal reconstructive surgery. Dines also argues that female performers may suffer from post-traumatic stress disorder (PTSD). As rosebudding (pushing the rectum out of the anus or "extreme anal") has moved from gay porn to mainstream straight performance, debates about the physical risk have correspondingly ensued. Side effects can include loosened rectal walls, bowel leakage, or there are no problems at all. Dines uses prolapse to argue about the extreme harms of pornography. However, the overall rate of rectal prolapse is relatively rare, with 2.5 cases per 100,000 people; and there is no clear-cut cause for it. Jeffrey Morken, MD, explains that prolapse may be uncomfortable and quite embarrassing; and it often has a significant negative impact on patients' quality of life, although it rarely results in an emergency medical situation. Rectal prolapse is treatable by surgery, albeit a medical intervention more commonly performed on the elderly.

Sexually transmitted infections are also a workplace consideration unique to porn (and other sex work). Even with routine STI testing and condom use, there is still a small risk of blood-borne pathogen transmission. The risk of chlamydia and gonorrhea is higher. Both are medically treatable but require costly antibiotics. For any contracted infection, there is the financial impact of missed bookings and the unquantifiable cost of emotional worry.

## Do Porn Performers Enjoy Having Sex for the Camera?

Again, as with any job, there are those who are strictly in it for the money, others who absolutely love their work, and some who are wildly exploited or trafficked into porn. Excluding victims of criminal trafficking, just like for employees and independent contractors outside the adult industry, some workdays are better than others.

When asked about the sex she had while doing porn, former performer Vanessa Belmond said 99 percent of the time sex on camera was not fun. In her words, porn sex is meant to look good, not feel good. It's a performance, fantasy, and illusion. Belmond left the sex industry when she was twenty-five, after seven years in the business. In Belladonna's 2003 *Primetime* interview with Diane Sawyer, the performer described feeling physically revolted during sex scenes. "My whole entire body feels it when I'm doing it and . . . I feel . . . so gross." Belladonna told Sawyer that while she was pretending to enjoy sex on camera, she was actually telling herself, "Hey, I only have this much time left. Don't worry about it. Get the check. Gonna go deposit it in your bank." Belladonna subsequently recanted several of her on-screen comments, claiming that ABC manipulated the footage. Years after the *Primetime* show, a *Vice* magazine "Skinema" video released in 2014 described Belladonna's initial foray into pornography not as glamorous but as sad and destructive.

In contrast, BBW adult actress April Flores says that her experience—and that of her colleagues—is overwhelmingly positive. "Everyone I've met is empowered, business-minded, and enjoys the work," Flores shares of her professional experience. In her ten years doing porn, Flores only met one person who admitted that they did not like performing, and that person retired soon after. As for potential injury, Flores reminds that working in pornography is a very physical job. As with any physical work, there can be injuries, which is why it is important to be careful and professional. On top-level shoots, there is a privilege of not being put in dangerous positions. Scenes are negotiated before you start shooting, Flores explains. These negotiations go beyond pay rate to include specifics about the scene such as tone, expectations, and whether there will be verbal conversations on camera. When you work with professional, experienced people, Flores says, you can always say no to a scene. In contrast, amateur—or inexperienced—porn production involves less professional preparation and can incur risk. "Answering a Craigslist ad and showing up at a random hotel is possibly dangerous for anyone," Flores points out.

Asked what she makes of the suggestion that porn performers are forced to say they like their work to appease their bosses or their fans, April Flores replies, "That is simply not true." These days, the pay rates are lower, performers have to test more often, and there simply is not enough money to stay in the adult industry if you don't like it. For those who continue working in porn, the money simply isn't what it used to be, and people have to be very diversified to make a living. Many porn performers have day jobs in addition to working in the adult industry. "It costs money to do this work," Flores explains during a personal interview. Rates are down, pirating is up, and we are tested twice a month at a cost of at least $150 for each test. That means we pay at least $300 every month to work in porn, so you have to love it to keep doing it.

Ned Henry describes the appeal of working in front of the camera as a chance for him to be seen as an erotic, sexy object of desire; as more than what he calls a "headless stunt cock," which is the prevalent role for men in mainstream straight porn. Participating in the adult industry allowed Henry to come out as queer.

Sometimes people wonder whether the orgasms they see in porn are real. Asking whether porn orgasms are real is similar to asking whether explosions or stunts are real in mainstream movies. Sometimes they are; sometimes they aren't. The premise of pornography is that it is a performance. The actor's job is to make the scene appear authentic, accidental, or unscripted. The performer's primary goal is not intimacy or pleasure. Accidental intimacy can sometimes happen, but it is not the goal or the requirement of a porn production. On a fundamental level, Danny Wylde explains, the performer is doing work. Much like a professional athlete, this job involves exploiting his or her body for the entertainment of others in exchange for money.

It is not difficult for female performers to pretend they are having an orgasm. That is the role of an actor. To replicate ejaculate, Cetaphil soap and other concoctions replace actual semen in many of the still photographs. Annie Sprinkle, who made over 150 films during her 25-year porn career, has described in her one-woman show, "Post Porn Modernist," how she used Campbell's Cream of Mushroom Soup as a prop to replicate male ejaculate during oral sex scenes during her early film shoots.

### Why Do People Become Porn Performers?

Like any line of work, there are as many answers to this question as there are people working in porn. We often don't think of porn performers as everyday people with bills and children and student loans to pay off. In part, this is because the industry relies on cultivating performance and fantasy. As a condition of this fantasy, we are primarily accustomed to seeing adult performers in their "work clothes." This makes it easier to forget that pornography is a job.

The following is a sample of the variety of reasons why people become porn performers. Tobi Hill-Meyer, a multiracial trans activist, writer, and filmmaker, got into porn as a way to earn enough money for a 5,000-mile road trip to Camp Trans (started in 1991 as a protest to the exclusion of transwomen from the Michigan Womyn's Music Festival). "Fred" started work in porn as a BDSM submissive after his girlfriend and her mother introduced him to the industry. Lorelei Lee, who teaches writing at New York University and at the San

Francisco Center for Sex and Culture, started working in porn because she needed the money. Performer and educator Nina Hartley famously imparts the story about when her father found out what she does for a living. "He asked, 'Why sex? Why not the violin?' I know now," Hartley writes, "that I'm sexual the way that Mozart was musical . . . and a life of public sexuality has, from my very first time on stage, been as natural to me as breathing."[4]

Belle Knox, the first-year Duke University student who was outed as a porn performer when she was 19 years old, candidly responded to the media firestorm by explaining the high cost of college and how doing porn helped her pay for tuition. After doing erotic modeling, Stoya started in porn because she said it sounded like fun; and Dylan Ryan did her first shoot, in part, to help a friend launch her new porn company. Linda Boreman (aka Linda Lovelace, star of *Deep Throat*) describes being forced into the pornography business by her abusive husband, Chuck Traynor.

As with any job, there are various reasons why people go to work. The fact that financial need is a motivating factor should come as no shock whether the workplace is a restaurant or on the set of a porn shoot. Survival sex work is done for immediate, primary needs: food, clothing, shelter. Other financial motivations (tuition, travel, ongoing cash flow) may not be as stark as the difference between eating and going hungry, but money is still an important factor in the decision to do porn. For some, the choice to do porn is blended with curiosity, political statement, and sexual expression or exploration. For others who may be coerced or trafficked, there is no choice in entering this line of work.

*Hot Girls Wanted* is documentary about the steady stream of 18- to 21-year-olds entering the world of amateur pornography. "Pro-am" sites are among the most highly visited, and "teen" is the one of the most popular search terms for online pornography. Pro-am refers to professional adult actors pretending on camera to be young, newbie amateurs. But with the heavy demand for amateur, the documentary argues, the "girl next door" genre actually features young, exploited women who are naively looking for a way out of small-town life and maybe some adventure. Pro-am websites featuring brand new young women charge subscription fees for viewers. According to *Hot Girls Wanted*, the top three pro-am sites are worth an estimated $50 million, although no source for this figure is provided in the documentary.

The film emphasizes the "girls'" dead-end opportunities and search for fame. Critics, however, have noted that the documentary incorporates a story arc to make a point rather than simply and dispassionately reporting the facts. The working-class women featured in the documentary are juxtaposed with Belle Knox, the Duke University porn performer, thus pitting the two presumptively different socioeconomic classes against each other in a bid for which group has the most acceptable reasons for working in porn. The documentary suggests the reason young women start working in porn is because the media is saturated with hypersexualized images. According to the documentary, sexualized selfies are specifically to blame because their popularity promotes female self-objectification.

The documentary fails to acknowledge that wanting to leave a small town, where opportunities tend to be limited, has always been part of the American story. "People's reasons for running off to the Gold Rush, military service, or Hollywood are similar to these porn actresses' even if their job descriptions are different,"[5] writes Caitlin Cruz for *Talking Points Memo*. The documentary—and for that matter most commentary on the topic—does not explore the reasons why men start working in front of the camera.

Some men start in pornography for the adventure, for the money, for the job flexibility, or because they are trying to launch their acting careers. Some see porn as a way of reasserting their masculinity given that society equates successful gender performance with the appearance of virility.

## What Is the "Damaged Goods" Hypothesis?

The damaged goods hypothesis is one explanation that some people use to explain why women become porn performers. In sum, the claim is that women work in pornography because they were sexually abused as children, and they grow up to become drug addicts with a host of psychological problems. "Damaged goods" refers to stereotypes and perceptions—as opposed to verified professional assessments—that sex workers have low psychological health and self-esteem, with high rates of drug use and shame.

These negative stereotypes about women who work in adult entertainment are often used to condemn the pornography industry or to judge the women who work in it. Yet despite preconceived notions and political justifications built on these views, until recently, no study had been conducted to test the "damaged goods" hypothesis.

## Is This Hypothesis True?

In 2012, James Griffith, Sharon Mitchell, Christian Hart, Lea Adams, and Lucy Gu published the findings of a study they conducted to test the accuracy of the damaged goods hypothesis. The team wanted to know whether women in the adult industry would report harmful psychological traits and life experiences more often than women who are not porn performers. The four psychologists and one professional from the Adult Industry Medical Healthcare Foundation compared self-reports by 177 porn performers with a sample of women who were not porn performers, matching both groups in terms of age, ethnicity, and marital status.

The research team was interested in sexual behaviors and attitudes, self-esteem, quality of life, and drug use among porn actresses. Their findings, published in the *Journal of Sex Research*, found that compared to women outside the adult industry, female porn actors were more likely to identify as bisexual, experienced their first sexual encounter at a relatively early age, and had more sexual partners.

None of the factors, however, are automatically problems. On the face of it, if the women who have had these life experiences don't find them troubling, there is no reason to presume that they are. Whether one interprets bisexuality, early sexual encounters, or number of sexual partners as a problem may reflect conservative moral panic or religious views more so than proving that women in porn are "damaged."

Female performers were between three and nine times more likely than the matched group to have used ten different types of drugs (marijuana, hallucinogens, ecstasy, cocaine, heroin, other opiates, methamphetamine, tranquilizers, barbiturates, and other sedatives). It is important to note that these findings do not measure drug addiction but the rate at which participants ever tried or experimented with a drug. The only significant difference in terms of how often drugs were used in the six months prior to the survey revealed that marijuana was the only drug with a moderately higher use rate among porn actresses compared with women outside of porn.

Significantly, the comparison of porn performers and nonporn performers found no difference in the rate or incidence of childhood sexual abuse (CSA). This may be unfortunately due to the widespread sexual victimization of young girls across the board. About 36 percent of porn actresses reported being victims of childhood sexual assault; about 30 percent of the matched sample said they were victims of childhood sexual abuse. However, these findings certainly do not indicate a vastly lower rate of CSA among women outside of the pornography industry.

There are several limitations to the original study and the later investigation of the "damaged goods" hypothesis. First, the research focuses only on women. Although this is important, future studies will hopefully include male performers, and gender fluid or trans actors. Second, the research asks only whether participants experienced childhood sexual abuse.

The term is never clearly defined. There are more precise ways of assessing what can otherwise be a subjectively reported experience. Third, education may be an important factor in correlating the kinds of porn women engage in and the perceived options available to them. In any case, the assumptions and stereotypes that female porn performers are more likely to suffer from drug addiction and abuse is simply not true. The bottom line is that the damaged goods hypothesis is not supported by scientific research. In fact, when it came to measuring psychological characteristics, the porn actresses in this study had higher levels of self-esteem, positive feelings, social support, sexual satisfaction, and spirituality compared to the matched group of women who did not perform in pornography.

### What Are Some Concerns about Porn Performers' Well-Being?

Although it's fair to say that most people share their work (and their work stories) with family and friends, coming out as a porn performer can present unique challenges. In the Internet age, however, hiding what you do for work is unlikely (assuming that's even desired). Whereas some adult performers are accepted and supported by friends and family, others feel stigmatized and judged. For a performer to face well-intentioned concerns about their safety and well-being is not unusual.

Among the assumptions that are sometimes made is that porn performers lack education and are incapable of intellectual pursuits, that they don't have appropriate personal boundaries, or that they will do anything sexual for money.

In her anti-pornography work, author Gail Dines makes repeated references to the "body-punishing sex" women experience in making pornography and the ways in which ejaculate in porn marks women as used goods who are owned by the men who just penetrated them. In Dines' interpretation, "porn plays out 'fantasy' sex that looks more like sexual assault than making love." Women in pornography are penetrated in every orifice by any number of men, says Dines. Their bodies, like ours, have real physical limits, "yet the goal of the movie is to see just how far these limits can be pushed. At some point during all the pounding, her vagina will become sore, her anus raw and swollen, and her mouth will ache from having large penises thrust in and out for an extended amount of time." During this assault, she is called all kinds of vile names, and she has to look like she's enjoying it.[6]

In contrast, Lorelei Lee describes her own firsthand experience working in porn, noting that ideas about economic coercion or concern about women performing extreme sexual acts presumes that (a) performers are inherently devalued by pornography in a way that cannot be compensated by their earnings and that (b) no woman wants to have "that kind of sex." In Lorelie Lee's experience, her on-camera performances didn't become interesting to her until she created scenes that were physically challenging, such as fisting, double penetration, or anal sex. These are acts that are labeled "extreme" or "hard-core." But while some negatively judge these terms, Lee finds pushing her physical limits is, what she calls, a thing of physical beauty.

Other concerns are that performers face racist hatred, are sexually victimized on set, or are sex trafficked and forced into pornography. (I take up these issues in more detail in later chapters.) There are concerns that people working in the adult industry cannot have intimate, honest relationships with their partners or families. Again, as human beings, porn performers bring a wide range of personal history and experiences to the workplace and back to their homes. Two books— *Off the Set: Porn Stars and Their Partners* and *Coming Out Like a Porn Star*—document the rich and complicated relationships among porn performers, their families, and their intimate partners.

### How Do Performers Transition out of the Adult Industry?

Transitioning out of porn performing happens in all sorts of ways. Some people get married or move away; others go back to school; and some move behind the scenes writing scripts, directing, or becoming makeup artists.

Michelle Sinclair, who achieved significant renown as Belladonna, told *Vice*, "Since I retired three years ago it's been a trip. I don't know if it's like this for any other girl who leaves the adult industry, but for me, I'm trying to find myself.... I've thought about the sex-positive speaker route but I've also thought about a lot of things ... I feel like I'm at the place where most people are when they're just out of college, or getting ready to go to college, and figuring out what it is they really want to do with their lives." Still, she says, "I don't want to be typecast and I don't want to be naked, which is what most people would want to cast me for"[7] in mainstream films.

In writer and porn actress Stoya's opinion, having sex on camera is still highly stigmatized work. It negatively affects employment options later in life for many people. Yet anything she imagines herself doing in transitioning from the industry is going to be connected to her past, and to her experience and visibility in pornography, she says. According to Jeremy Steele, star of *Naughty Neighbors* and *M.I.L.F. Money*, one of the hardest things about working in porn is trying to reinvent yourself if you leave the industry. If people find out that you were a sex worker on film or video, Steele reports to *Forbes*, "you can lose a job or not find one if you're too well known for having been a whore on camera, in spite of it being legal."[8] April Flores has a different perspective: we live in the twenty-first century, not in the past. At this point everyone has engaged in sexual media in some way, whether through sexting, naked selfies, or homemade porn video for personal use. This idea that working in porn is stigmatizing is antiquated, and it will phase out. It's just not a big deal, says Flores. "Especially in a big city. Everyone's done something."

# 5

# WHO'S WATCHING PORN?

Myths and stereotypes about sexuality are common. This misinformation also applies when it comes to questions about who is watching porn—and why. There is a lot of research exploring these issues; but as for solid conclusions, the jury is still out.

The question about who is watching porn, how often, and of what variety is significant for several reasons. Understanding general patterns in social behavior informs our understanding about society's trends and norms. If there are countries or regions that claim to be sexually conservative, yet the region's porn use patterns reveal something different, this raises an interesting rhetoric and reality gap. Second, pornography is at the center of legal and moral questions. If we are concerned about children or teenagers accessing pornography, then accurate demographic data helps inform our policies and conclusions about the best plans to implement.

Other questions about gender politics, infidelity and porn use, or sexual fantasy and sexual orientation are also addressed through understanding who is watching pornography. Research that investigates the impact of porn use on viewers also relies on knowing who's watching. Yet, like so many other aspects of sexual behavior, porn use data is often shrouded in myth or simply difficult to ascertain.

## *Is It True that Men Are More Visually Aroused than Women?*

In a word, the answer to this question is *No*. Although conventional wisdom often repeats the dictum that men are more visual creatures than women, the research does not convincingly support this stereotype. A common assumption, however, is that men are more likely to watch porn because, compared with women, men are sexually aroused by visual cues. To clear up the confusion, a bit of foundational information about gender research is helpful.

Evolutionary psychologists and self-appointed experts claim that nature creates sexual attraction, and the roots of our sex drive go back to the Stone Age. *Penthouse* magazine's publisher Bob Guccione told *ABC News* that men are simply biologically wired to enjoy looking at sexy women. "This may be very politically incorrect," Guccione pronounced, "but that's the way it is . . . It's all part of our ancestral conditioning." Feminist writer Katha Pollitt counters that human sexual behavior cannot be reduced to this this sort of evolutionary, biological assumption. Homosexuality is hard to explain as a biological adaptation. So is stamp collecting, says Pollitt. And, it stands to reason, presumably so is porn. "We pursue countless passions that have no direct bearing on survival" or on the evolution of the species, Pollitt explains.[1]

In what Christopher Ryan and Cacilda Jethá refer to in their book *Sex at Dawn* as "the standard narrative of human sexual evolution," the story about heterosexual coupling is that men and women choose a sexual partner based on their mate value and their reproductive capacities. She looks for signs of wealth; he looks for fertility—signs that many researchers claim are indicated by factors such as childbearing hips and a robust breast. As this just-so story goes, this so-called hard-wired drive creates men's biologically heightened tendency to be sexually turned on by visual cues. This would supposedly explain why men like porn. Yet, it's worth noting, as Ryan and Jethá suggest, that using evolutionary psychology to explain human sexuality does not explain the popular themes available in mainstream heterosexual pornography.

If biology is destiny, and if men's competitive drive to have their sperm win the reproductive race explains their visually driven sexual behavior, then how can we explain the popularity of mainstream, gangbang porn featuring a group of men having sex with one woman? Using evolutionary psychology to explain who is using porn, and what kind, falls short when it comes to male-on-female group sex or for the cuckold scenes that are consistently popular fantasies among married men.

Like the biased assumption that men are more visual creatures, an additional stereotype is that women prefer watching romantic scenes instead of seeing overt sex that lacks relationships among the participants. Researchers testing for this pattern expected to find that men would show a stronger preference for sexual stimuli and that women would express a strong preference for romantic stimuli. They were amazed to find that both men and women showed stronger automatic preferences for romantic stimuli compared to content with strictly sexual content. But what would account for the discrepancies between conventional assumptions and actual research findings when it comes to stereotypes about gender and porn?

According to psychologist Cordelia Fine, author of *Delusions of Gender*, a great deal of research shows that people respond with gender-stereotyped behavior when they are given gender-stereotyped prompts. What's more, stereotype-primed men tend to perform higher, and women who are primed with stereotypically feminine prompts tend to drop in their ability to perform various visual and spatial tasks. Due to what's called the stereotype threat, this is especially true when researchers tell men that they perform better than women on the tasks they are then asked to complete.

In other words, the assumption that men are more visual creatures and are therefore "naturally" drawn to pornography can be explained by evolutionary psychology or common assumptions, but it can't be explained *well*. The research evidence about whether attraction to porn is hardwired is often far more shaky than is often presumed.

What all of this means is that in addition to the challenges of collecting data—particularly when it comes to something so personal as using pornography—gender stereotypes often further skew our ability to gather and understand the demographic information about who is watching porn. Women, for instance, are still far less likely to self-report their porn use given the stereotypes and stigma about gender and sexuality that exist in so many cultures. The term for this data collection problem is social desirability bias.

### What Are the Demographics on Porn Use?

Pornography is available in a variety of formats including books, comics, manga, or magazines. A 2004 Norwegian study found that 76 percent of adults had seen porn magazines, 67 percent had seen X-rated movies, and 24 percent had watched Internet porn. According to a US Congressional report commissioned in the same year, 70 million individuals visited porn sites every week. However, the Pew Research Center indicates that in 2013, only 12 percent of adult Internet users in the United States spent time watching sexually explicit content.

Looking at the pool of porn users somewhat differently, data collected by Vocativ and Pornhub reveals that as a percentage of all porn users, women ages 18–24 watch 5 percent more porn than their male counterparts.

Regardless of who is watching, the question about whether porn is acceptable differs by education, religion, and age. A broad overview of the data reveals some interesting patterns. People with advanced degrees are a bit more likely than college graduates to think it is morally acceptable to watch porn (40 and 34 percent, respectively). But both college grads and those with advanced degrees are significantly more likely than high school graduates to approve of watching pornography.

When it comes to religion and race or ethnicity, white Catholics are twice as likely as Hispanic Catholics to report that watching porn is morally acceptable (28 and 14 percent, respectively). Of white evangelical Protestants, 88 percent claim they have moral objections to viewing pornography; whereas by comparison, only 40 percent of religiously unaffiliated people express moral concerns about porn.

When it comes to age factors, it appears that the older you are, the less likely you approve of porn. Of Millennials, 45 percent think watching porn is morally okay while 33 percent of people aged 34–48 have no moral objection to porn, and only 9 percent of those over the age of 68 approve of watching pornography. In one of the few studies investigating porn use by women *and* men, German researchers found that Millennial women were active and interested porn consumers. These women used porn to stimulate their own sexual desire and did not express disinterest or disgust. But if we know what folks *think* about porn, the question still remains: who is watching?

### How Does Age Make a Difference?

Between 2009 and 2013, the share of American online adults who watched or downloaded any kind of video grew from 69 percent of Internet users to 78 percent. Compared with the 58 percent of online users watching comedy or humor videos, the 12 percent of American adults watching porn reported by Pew seems wildly low. There are signs, however, that online porn use differs by age.

Whereas the Pew study found that only 4 percent of adults over 50 watched adult videos, this figure jumped to 25 percent among 18- to 29-year-olds. Much of the research indicates a gender gap in addition to an age gap. According to Pew, men are much heavier consumers of online porn; their report claims that 25 percent of viewers are male and only 8 percent are female. In a Swedish study conducted by Sven-Axel Månsson, there was a distinct tendency for the viewing habits among men and women to converge among the younger age groups when it comes to using online pornography. Although only 4 percent of women between the ages of 50 and 65 said they watched Internet porn, this figure jumped to approximately 25 percent of the women aged 18 to 34 who reported having done the same.

Clarissa Smith, Martin Barker, and Feona Attwood had similar findings published in *New Views on Pornography*. By cross-tabulating gender and age, Smith, Barker, and Attwood found that younger women (18 to 25) engage with pornography much more often than older women. These figures could mean a variety of things. First, they may indicate a generational shift, with younger cohorts growing up in a world where they are more comfortable watching porn. Second, the data could indicate that younger adults watch more porn, with this figure dropping off as they get older. Third, there is the distinct possibility that younger adults are more comfortable self-reporting their online porn use to researchers, which would skew the results accordingly.

Research conducted by Månsson further showed that three-fourths of the women who had watched pornography during the preceding year had done so in the company of their male partner. Månsson suggests that women's pornography consumption might be related to their male partners' pornography consumption patterns. These patterns may also indicate the cultural permission that men have to be sexual and the slut-shaming risk that inhibits women's freedom to claim their own sexual pleasure. Given that Månsson's research was published in 2000, it is possible these gendered dichotomies are shifting over time. Research conducted in Australia found evidence that a growing proportion of porn consumers are women. In Catharine Lumby' s 2008 book *The Porn Report*, the media scholar found empirical evidence that a growing proportion of those watching porn are women. Indeed, in

2009, women reportedly comprised 56 percent of business at *Hustler*'s stores, with Candida Royalle's videos, made specifically for female viewers, selling 10,000 copies a month.

When asked *why* they view porn, respondents to Smith, Barker, and Attwood's study had a range of answers: "It's not a habit but something to enjoy occasionally"; "Well, I don't need to view pornography for gratification—my own imagination is far better. It's great for when you are just horny and lazy however!"; "It's less that porn is important and more that it is nice to have. Were I to lose it tomorrow the funeral would be short but it would be missed." Others cited voyeurism, old age, exploration, boredom, or lack of a sex partner as reasons why they used erotic material.

### How Many People Watch Porn While They're at Work?

Several news stories report instances of employees using porn at work. According to the *Boston Herald*, a top cardiologist at Massachusetts General Hospital was required to register as a sex offender and lost his medical license after downloading copious amounts of child pornography onto his work computer. In another child pornography case involving the workplace, the Associated Press reports that a businessman was charged with possessing child pornography after a photo of a nude boy appeared during a PowerPoint presentation. James Andrew Smith was fired from his job upon this discovery and also stepped down as pastor of Landmark Baptist Church. The *Chicago Sun-Times* reported allegations of police officers viewing pornography on department computers, resulting in online tracking and Internet software to prevent access to 500,000 blocked websites.

Spectacular violations of workplace protocol and the law notwithstanding, viewing pornography at work is somewhat commonplace. A poll conducted by Harris Interactive and Qumu.com shows that about 3 percent of Americans *admit* to watching pornography while at work. The actual numbers are higher. The Nielson Company found in 2010 that nearly 30 percent of American workers accessed porn during work, with an average length of 12 minutes and 38 seconds per viewing session. A CNBC report places this figure much higher, with 70 percent of all online porn access reportedly taking place during the nine-to-five workday.

As the economy crashed after the 2008 Great Recession, US government workers came under specific scrutiny for their on-the-job porn use. As CNBC put it, senior agency staffers at the Securities and Exchange Commission (SEC) spent hours surfing porn websites on government-issued computers while they were supposed to be policing America's financial system. A senior attorney at the SEC headquarters spent up to eight hours a day downloading porn. When he ran out of hard drive space, he burned files to CDs and DVDs that he kept in boxes around his office. An SEC accountant was blocked more than 16,000 times in one month from visiting porn websites, yet he managed a workaround to collect porn using Google Images, which bypassed the SEC's internal filter. By 2010, there were 31 inquiries into SEC employees watching porn on the job. Among these, 17 were senior-level employees earning salaries up to about $200,000.[2]

In 2013, Covenant Eyes, a Christian anti-pornography company that provides accountability and filtering software, compiled the following data regarding porn use in organizations, dating back roughly ten years. In a survey of human resources professionals, two-thirds said they have discovered pornography on employee computers. Nearly half of those said they had found such material more than once. A 2004 study of 350 companies in the United States, the United Kingdom, and Australia found that one-third of workers admitted passing along porn to coworkers. The July 25, 2005, issue of *Computerworld* reported that half of Fortune 500 companies had dealt with at least one incident related to computer porn over a 12-month period. Offenders were fired in 44 percent of these incidents, and an additional 41 percent faced disciplinary action.

By 2014, survey data revealed that 63 percent of men and 36 percent of women were watching porn while they were at work. Three-fourths of men between ages 31 to 49, and also men earning more than $75,000 a year, reported that they watch porn at work. Close to 50 percent of women in the same age range also said they cruised porn sites on the job. It is worth observing that the porn-use data is often collected by the adult industry or by companies profiting from the sale of porn filtering software and other similar products. In this case, Proven Men Industries, a group that opposes pornography and sells filtering software, also collected the data regarding porn use at work.

### What Is the Data on Men and Women Watching Porn?

Studies published in the *Journal of Adolescent Research* and the *Archives of Sexual Behavior* found that nearly nine out of ten young adult men use pornography, whereas only one-third of women reported doing the same. As PornResearch.org comments, the findings about who is watching porn don't contain many surprises, "aligning as they do with popular understandings of pornography as predominately a heterosexual male pastime." That said, there are notable gender distinctions in the frequency of porn use, what kind of porn is used, and the motivation for watching it.

According to the authors of "Generation XXX," the majority of young adult women (18 to 26) said they only used porn once a month or less. Only 3.2 percent of women reported that they watch porn weekly or more. In contrast, 50 percent of young men use porn weekly.[3] When it comes to the type of content men and women seek out, very few online porn users mindlessly click on "pop-ups," the images that interrupt intentional browsing to lead viewers to other sites. This is significant because the evidence indicates that porn consumers are not simply opportunistic or indiscriminate media users. It appears that porn does not seek out viewers (as some critics claim);

rather, consumers actively pursue the sexually explicit materials they choose to engage with. As Clarissa Smith, Martin Barker, and Feona Attwood found in their research on why people use porn, online users have "rich histories and tastes, which connect in complex ways with [their] understandings of sex and sexuality in their everyday lives."[4]

Tube sites are the most frequently viewed sources of porn for both women and men. Downloads and amateur sites are twice as popular among men than they are for women. And, among all users, the top-five most popular forms of porn are specialist sites, meaning they cater to specific sexual interests.

When it comes to reading online porn fiction (as compared to watching videos), this genre has way more appeal for women. Women click on porn fiction at nearly double the rate at which men choose these sites. Although these results may seem to uphold the old stereotypes that women are more interested in words about sex and men prefer pictures, Smith, Barker, and Attwood explain that if we consider these findings in relation to their results regarding orientations toward pornography, there are more finely developed patterns. Their research results "suggest that there are some broad, general differences between men's and women's orientations to porn. For example, men seem more inclined to use porn simply to *express* their arousal, but women are more likely to use pornography as a *means to arousal*. Women also seem to engage with porn as a means to reconnect with their bodies, and to use with partners. Men seem more likely to turn to pornography when feeling bored or having nothing better to do."[5]

### What Is the Data on Couples Watching Porn Together?

In one of the few studies looking at porn and relationships, Kristian Danebac, Bente Træen, and Sven-Axel Månsson surveyed heterosexual couples asking about their use of pornography. In only 3 percent of the Norwegian couples surveyed, the female partner had used pornography, on her own, in any form including movies, magazines, or the Internet. In 5 percent of the couples, only the male partner had used pornography. In 15 percent of the couples, both partners had used pornography to enhance their sex lives. The researchers surmise "pornography is primarily a solitary activity for most Norwegians," explaining that "it is not part of the interpersonal sexual script applied to guide sexual conduct between committed lovers."[6]

However, when it came to accessing Internet pornography (as compared to a broader variety of sources), Danebac, Træen, and Månsson found that 36 percent of the men and 6 percent of the women reported using online porn. Whereas 4 percent of couples claimed they'd both watched Internet porn, a total of 62 percent of couples said they used no online porn at all. A further breakdown of the data began to show a gendered pattern in porn use among couples. In one-third of the couples, the man had watched pornography on the Internet alone; only 2 percent of couples claimed that the woman had done this. About half of the men and nearly 60 percent of the women solo porn users said their partners knew about their online activities. The men whose partners knew they watched online porn also said it was easy for them to talk with their partner about sex.

Based on the data, Danebac, Træen, and Månsson suggest that pornography use is primarily a solitary activity, although this finding probably isn't astonishing. Among couples, porn use was seen as relatively unacceptable for those in committed love relationships. In part, the authors suggest, this is because porn use by couples requires active decisions, discussions, and negotiations that may be quite difficult in an environment where sexuality and pornography is shrouded in silence.

### How Does Porn Use Correlate to Religious and Political Views?

When it comes to the demographic data about who uses porn, there is often a rhetoric and reality gap between what people say and what they do. The Public Religion Research Institute

(PPRI) finds that only 29 percent of Americans overall think watching porn is morally acceptable. That said, on closer inspection, a curious pattern emerges in the research. Findings reported by *Discover* magazine in 2014 reveal that people in highly religious and conservative states seek out more online pornography than their more liberal neighbors.

Over a two-year period, Cara C. MacInnis and Gordon Hodson found that in highly religious and conservative states, there is also a correspondingly high volume of Internet searches for sexual content. This association between religious conviction, political conservatism, and the search for online porn is a moderate to strong one. In a scatterplot indicating correlations between religiosity and Google searches for sex, conservative Mississippi ranked the highest, whereas Vermont—known to be a liberal state—clocked in with the lowest number of both Internet searches and religiosity. Just knowing the number of conservatives in a given state was enough information for the researchers to accurately predict the extent of pornography searches using key words including sex, gay sex, porn, free porn, XXX, and gay porn. These findings held true even after the researchers controlled for other demographic variables such as population size, poverty rate, and Internet use among various states. Harvard Business School professor Benjamin Adelman's research replicates these findings, with Utah and Mississippi ranking the highest rates of online porn site subscriptions.

Because people who believe in conservative political and religious ideology are generally associated with opposing homosexuality, sex outside marriage, and non-procreative sex, these findings might raise some eyebrows. There are a few plausible interpretations for the positive correlation between high rates of conservatism and the volume of US Internet porn searches. This paradox may result from preoccupation with sexual content, presumably because of the taboo. It may also be the case that high rates of online sexual activity come from liberals who live in these sexually restrictive right-leaning states.

MacInnis and Hodson's research question forms the title of their article, "Do American States With More Religious or Conservative Populations Search More for Sexual Content on Google?" Their affirmative finding "offers rich and meaningful insights into the largely private lives of Americans, revealing their natural interests." As MacInnis and Hodson state, however, their research concerned religiosity and conservatism in the United States, which is a predominantly Christian nation, with a highly polarized left–right political divide. It remains an open question as to whether similar associations exist outside of the American context.[7]

### What Is the Data on Global Porn Use?

PornMD is an online search engine connected to Pornhub, which also hosts the data-collecting site "Insights." Vocativ, a digital media company that tracks and publishes trending online stories and videos, has also teamed up with Pornhub to collect data regarding online porn viewing patterns. The Pornhub database is robust, although there are two significant concerns. First, the Pornhub data set is a measure of users accessing one particular tube site: their own. Still, these figures should provide general indicators and a snapshot of global online porn use. Second, Pornhub is a group of video sharing websites that post video clips and often pirated porn. (For more on the issue of stolen porn, see chapter 3.) Although there are serious legal and ethical issues raised by their business practices (and their use of derogatory terms such as "shemale"), Pornhub and PornMD are able to track global demographic patterns thanks to the high volume of Internet traffic clicking through the site. In addition, PornMD's live-search site tracks online keyword searches in real time.[8]

Each month, the site aggregates the top keyword searches and then organizes these terms by continent or by region. A look at these results for April 2015 provides a snapshot of global Internet searches for porn. Among the global top ten searches, compilation, teen, MILF (Mothers I'd Like to Fuck), hentai, and anal rank in the top five. The remaining keyword searches in the global top ten include amateur, mom and son, Japanese, mom, and POV (Point of View).

These keywords remain largely the same around the world, with slight additions or deletions across various regions. For instance, "backroom casting couch" appears specifically in the United States top ten searches; Canada favors MFC (Mildly Fat Chick) and Asian; China's top ten terms include Japanese and kung fu porn; fake taxi is popular in Italy and Libya; hijab makes the list in Algeria; and mothers turn up as top terms among porn searches in Iraq. Brazil specifically favors the performer Julia Paes; Anikka Albrite is a favorite in Peru; and Madison Ivy is heavily viewed in Sweden.

Among global searches that are specified as gay, daddy, bear, chub, grandpa, bareback, and twink are common top ten terms. Interestingly, "straight" is among the most frequently used search terms for people watching gay porn in Russia. Across the board, popular search terms shift with age. Whereas 20-somethings are more likely to seek out "stepmom," at around age 45 the term "massage" first appears in the top five keyword searches. In the 55–64 age cohort, "massage" jumps to the number one search term and "stepmom" drops to number three. In terms of the length of time spent online, the annual global average in 2013 was approximately eight hours. The United States came in first with an annual use of just over ten hours; the United Kingdom and France were both a close second, with about nine hours of online porn use per year. Japan, Spain, and Brazil all ranked at about seven hours of online porn viewing for the year. Using phones to access porn increased around the globe; and, in some countries such as Mexico and the UK, phone access equaled or surpassed computer use.

Analyzed by age, it appears that the younger adults around the world (ages 25–34) spend just under nine minutes at a time watching porn videos. This length of time grows longer as users get older, with those 65 and up spending just over ten minutes per visit. Monday is the most popular day for watching porn around the globe, perhaps coinciding with the data regarding the large number of folks accessing adult content while they are at work.

## How Is This Demographic Information Collected?

Industry sources such as *Xbiz* and *Adult Video News* track demographic trends regarding porn use including magazine and DVD sales. As of 2015, there was only one systematic attempt to determine how much of the Internet was comprised of adult content. According to one study at the behest of the US Department of Justice, Berkeley professor of statistics Philip Stark found that about 6 percent of online searches were for sexual content, and only about 1 percent of all websites indexed by Google and Microsoft were porn sites. Although this percentage is low, the raw numbers still amount to millions of websites devoted to porn; and, as *The Guardian* points out in asking "Just how much pornography is there online?," this percentage does not account for the sites that evade indexing.

Neuroscientists Ogi Ogas and Sai Gaddam took issue with Stark's method of sampling websites. Instead of measuring a random sample of online sites, the co-authors of *A Billion Wicked Thoughts* instead looked at the million most popular websites in the world. They found that 4 percent of all websites were based on adult content. The researchers also had a hunch that sampling the top one million online sites would provide a more realistic indication of a random person's experience with pornography on the Internet. Ogas and Gaddam explain that the two best metrics for analyzing the level of human interest in sex on the Internet is first, how often people freely search for it and second, what amount of web traffic goes to porn sites. Using these metrics, they found that about 10 to 15 percent of the Internet is porn. (These are higher than Stark's findings, but still a much lower figure than other, sometimes sensationalized, claims made by conservative anti-porn groups.)

### What Are the Challenges in Data Collection?

One significant challenge in collecting data regarding porn use is simply that it is hard to track. A second challenge is that people can be reluctant to self-disclose about such an intimate subject. Third, although measurements such as Internet keyword searches can be counted and analyzed, what's missing are the number of multiple users who may be accessing the site together, or repeat access to one porn source that is downloaded and watched multiple times after the initial keyword search. Similarly, circulation figures for magazines and books can be quantified; but knowing how many people buy a magazine is not exactly the same thing as knowing how many people read the issue, how many times it was read, or which particular images or stories in a single magazine attracted (or repelled) consumers. In addition, the politics that surround porn research often result in competing claims when it comes to interpreting the data.

It could easily be the case that the amount of porn use reported by Covenant Eyes, and other anti-pornography sources, are simply exaggerated. According to *Forbes*, it's not always clear how researchers decide that a website is pornographic. If the folks doing the research also have Internet filtering software to sell, it may be that their reported figures are overstated. Sociologist Ronald Weitzer suggests that researchers who use an "oppression paradigm" end up with skewed information because the setup for data collection presupposes that exploitation and violence are central to pornography. Instead, accurately collecting data requires recognizing (1) porn's immensely variegated content, (2) the range of ways consumers engage with porn, and (3) the possibility that pornography might enhance people's sex lives and intimate relationships. Anti-pornography researchers often set aside these foundational research principles to prove that the genre is always harmful and utterly without redeeming value. This perspective, Weitzer explains, skews the analysis and potentially impacts public policy and law enforcement.[9]

Research methods also impact data collection. In Ana Bridges's article about aggression in best-selling pornography, a research team conducted a content analysis of best-selling pornography videos to assess the level of violence toward women. They found high levels of verbal and physical aggression in these videos. Notably, variables such as spanking and hair pulling were coded as violent acts, but it's not at all clear that these activities are inherently harmful or even violent. In the Bridges study, ATM (ass-to-mouth) scenes were depicted in 41 percent of scenes, and gagging appeared in nearly 54 percent. This is presented "as an inherently degrading practice" without further discussion about whether—or if—this is always the case. Although this research investigates porn content rather than who's watching it, the findings are related. Effects research is a field that assesses the impact of pornography (or other media) on its viewers. In Bridges's case, the assumption is that pornography promotes violence against women, that porn viewers will be lulled into believing rape myths, and that porn consumers learn to associate aggression with pleasure.

An additional problem in data collection is described by the authors of "Generation XXX," who note that a lot of the existing literature about pornography use is limited. Researchers often measure use patterns with response codes that are open to individuals' interpretation (e.g., never, seldom, sometimes, often). More precise survey categories would provide actual frequencies of use (e.g., weekly, every other day, daily), which would more accurately assess how often people use porn and thus result in far more meaningful research findings.

Research by Alan Mckee on the links between pornography and sexual aggression makes a different case about the effects on viewers, one that speaks to the challenge in collecting data.

In McKee's view, researchers studying the effects of porn depend on dubious methods of sampling and data gathering. The connection made between exposure to pornography and increases in misogyny and aggression depend on a number of contingencies such as (1) being able to expose large numbers of people to pornography that (2) they had not selected under (3) uncomfortable conditions (surrounded and observed by strangers) and that (4) prohibited normal reactions (i.e., masturbation). McKee reasons that the structure of the experiments, not the pornography itself, is what upsets people. Being asked to watch porn you didn't choose, in laboratory-type settings, among strangers and without being able to masturbate privately, is enough to make anyone angry, he surmises. The main thing this type of research actually reveals is that exposure to pornography *in experiments* makes people angry.[10]

### How Might Stigma and Stereotypes about Gender Impact the Data on Who Uses Porn?

The Pew Research Center found that only 12 percent of adult Internet users in the United States spent time watching porn. The research was conducted by phone, and Pew acknowledges that the small 12 percent figure may better account for people's reluctance to report their behavior rather than accurately measuring actual adult online porn use.[11] Or, as a *Time* magazine headline humorlessly put it, "12 Percent of Americans Admit to Watching Porn Online, the Other 88 Percent Must Not Have Internet." As the *Time* subtitle further explains, "Bashful survey respondents probably diminished the total reported number of online porn watchers in the U.S."[12] Shame and stigma could be a factor in this. The Public Religion Research Institute found that 71 percent of Americans think watching pornography is immoral. Yet moral objection to porn doesn't necessarily stop people from watching. Moral concerns may mean people watch porn but feel guilty doing so.

Just as Pew Research notes that some adults may be unwilling to share whether or how much they watch porn, this reluctance is likely more pronounced for women. In *I Am Not a Slut*, author Leora Tanenbaum explains that slut shaming—using supposed promiscuity as a deep insult—functions as a huge form of social policing over girls and women's sexuality (efforts to reclaim the term "slut" notwithstanding). Surely, it is not hard to imagine that a culture of slut shaming would have a deterrent effect on girls and women admitting they use porn, enjoy pornography, or have even taken a peek out of curiosity.

Writing about the Pew research for *Slate*, journalist Amanda Hess deduces that if we think the figures for male video viewership are low—and that men are reluctant to admit to Pew over the phone that they watch porn—then it stands to reason that women would be particularly unlikely to openly describe the details of their online porn habits given the risk of slut shaming and the fact that women are repeatedly told that porn is just for men.

At the same time, given the social scripts that meld masculinity with sexual prowess, it stands to reason that men may be more likely to overreport how much porn they watch. In 2009, researchers at the University of Montreal made headlines when they announced that they had attempted to study the impact of pornography on young men's sexuality but could not find a control group. In other words, the scientists were unable to find men in their twenties who had not seen porn. Whereas the researchers concluded that all men have seen porn, an alternative conclusion could also be that no men would want to admit they'd never seen it.

# 6

# PLEASURE AND DANGER IN PORNOGRAPHY

From the figures on revenue and use rates, to considerations about pornography's impact on viewers, the experts do not quite agree about what is going on with patterns and trends. Research about whether porn causes harm and measures of how much violence appears in porn is contentious. The jury is still out on the impact of pornography on people's sense of self, on men's perceptions of women, and on women's perceptions of themselves and of men. There is ongoing concern about misogyny, transphobia, and racism in the images the mainstream porn industry produces. There are those who argue that pornography is the result of human trafficking, although there is evidence the claims about global sex trafficking— although concerning—are exaggerated. For every finding that shows pornography causes harm or creates negative effects, there is another contradictory study. For all of the data proving that evidence of pornography's harms are overblown, or that pornography has positive social value, there is a political group ready to argue the point. It's been said that the one thing pornography is actually known to cause is masturbation.

### Does Pornography Cause Violence against Women?

In her book *Anti-Porn*, London-based author Julia Long refers to the abuse experienced by women working in pornography.

Long argues that women cannot possibly enjoy a production defined by repeated sexual use of their bodies and, in particular, body-punishing penetration. Similarly, the first-person testimony of violence by female performers such as Linda Lovelace (who starred in *Deep Throat*) led Andrea Dworkin to argue that pornography *is* violence. Or, as feminist Robin Morgan famously said, "Pornography is the theory, and rape is the practice." Sociologist Gail Dines argues that pornography grooms men to masturbate to eroticized images of women being harmed.

In making such statements about pornography and sexual harm, Julia Long, Andrea Dworkin, Robin Morgan, and others offer thoughtful insight about the danger and pervasiveness of sexism in everyday life. At the same time, the argument that pornography causes rape excludes questions about the possibility of sexual pleasure through porn and conflates causation with possible correlation. Recent studies about how people respond to pornography reveal a variety of effects, but none of these conclusively find that pornography causes rape.

As one might imagine, the debate between these groups is heated and contentious. The conversations around pleasure and danger in pornography are "two sets of discourses and arguments that are always in conversation with one another," says media scholar Lynn Comella. Juxtaposing these issues and concerns allows people "to see the degree to which the positions are much like a call and response, or an ongoing dialogue"—and a dialogue that often looks more like a street fight more than it does a civil conversation.

### What Are the Debates and the Data?

According to Gail Dines, those who watch modern pornography are becoming increasingly desensitized to the images and interactions they see on screen. In her words, soft-core porn no longer even exists because viewers are demanding increasingly more hard-core images. We are "entering a world of sexual cruelty where things that can be done to a woman to debase and dehumanize her, are sexualized," and this poses a danger to male sexuality and female safety. Dines says that growing up seeing cruel Internet pornography has a profound effect on the way boys and men "think about sex, relationships, intimacy, bodily integrity, and consent. Masturbating to porn that is a sometimes lethal mix of sex and violence [has] an intense effect on the body and mind."[1]

Not so fast, say Marleen Klaassen and Jochen Peter, researchers from the University of Amsterdam. Their porn study published in the *Journal of Sex Research* involved analyzing the content of 400 popular online porn videos aimed at heterosexual viewers. Their conclusion challenges the sweeping generalization that women in mainstream pornography are consistently dehumanized, subordinated, and harmed by men.

Klaassen and Peter's analysis measured features such as the power dynamics between sexual partners in porn videos, the amount of violence that appeared, and against whom that violence was directed. This research "made a distinct note of when people were objectified as being 'instrumental' to another's pleasure or being 'dehumanized' as having no thoughts or feelings,"[2] writes Alana Massey for *Pacific Standard*. After accounting for three main dimensions of gender inequality—objectification, power, and violence—Klaassen and Peter found that women and men in porn videos were equally portrayed as initiating sex and holding positions of power in the workplace (for those porn storylines that take place in the office or other employment sites). Although women were more often objectified through "instrumentality" with camera techniques using close-up shots of their bodies, men were more likely to be objectified through "dehumanization" by having their faces infrequently appearing on camera.

In Klaassen and Peter's research, men were more often shown as dominant and women as submissive during sexual activities; and although there was spanking and gagging, violence occurred infrequently, and nonconsensual sex was rare. A five-person team led by Ana Bridges found more dramatic instances of violence, aggression, and degradation in popular heterosexual porn videos. The authors claim theirs is the first study to track the increasing portrayal of sexual practices that are "potentially harmful to women in real life (and to the actresses in pornography videos), such as double penetration" and ass-to-mouth which the research team found in 41 percent of the scenes they watched. Citing Gail Dines to prove that ATM is "humiliating for women" (because Dines says so), the research findings further point to logistic regression analyses indicating that ATM scenes were a strong predictor of verbal aggression.[3]

Chyng Sun, a professor of media studies at New York University and director of the POV documentary, *The Price of Pleasure: Pornography, Sexuality and Relationships*, was also a member of the research team that found links between ATM and violence. Sun reports that instances of physical and verbal aggression were present in 90 percent of mainstream porn scenes they analyzed. Films directed by women are no less likely to contain aggression than films directed by men, she notes. Among the variables coded as violent are activities such as spanking, hair pulling, gagging, and name-calling. The research team's decision to categorize specific activities as violent is important to consider because (a) spanking or hair pulling, for instance, may not be considered violent by some people; (b) the concept of "verbal aggression" is open to interpretation given that one person's insult is another person's kink; and (c) there remains the question of force, impact, frequency, or degree of various actions. For instance, does all spanking constitute violence? Or is there a distinction between a tap on the ass and flogging? This research does not say.

While activist-scholars such as Chyng Sun argue that pornography's aggressive images are harmful and promote negative stereotypes about women, thereby encouraging actual violence, others disagree. Clinical sexologist Seth Prosterman reminds that research has failed to draw a clear connection between pornography and criminal sexual behavior. Instead of concluding that ATM or spanking causes harm, it is entirely plausible that in the case of criminal violence there are additional or intervening variables such as the presence of alcohol use. Attention to these additional variables in relation to pornography can potentially shed light on sexual violence and public safety issues.

In terms of content in porn videos, Klaassen and Peter found in their research that amateur pornography contained more overall gender inequality at women's expense when compared with professional porn. But given the diversity of material and wide range of genres available within pornographic media, they comment, it is intellectually and scientifically foolish to "assume implicitly that pornography is a homogenous mass of sexually explicit content" that always "promotes gender inequality because it treats women as sex objects, subordinates them, and depicts rape and violence against them."[4] Andy Ruddock, Senior Lecturer in Communications and Media Studies at Monash University, Australia, offers that various meta-analyses indicate that a connection between using pornography and expressing sexual aggression "was especially true if the pornography was violent, and if the viewer was a man already considered at risk of offending in this regard."

Anti-pornography researchers counter that even if pornography doesn't directly cause violence against women, it contributes to rape culture, a climate that eroticizes and trivializes sexual assault. At the suggestion that pornography is the root of rape culture, adult performer Stoya responded by telling HuffPost Live host Ricky Camilleri, "You know what promotes rape culture? Idiots promote rape culture. People who don't teach their children the difference between real life and things that you see in movies, and people who don't understand the difference between right and wrong."

Yet when Rape Crisis South London carried out simple research by typing the term "rape porn" in Google, their results showed that 86 percent of sites that came up advertised videos depicting the rape of women under the age of 18; 75 percent of sites involved guns or knives; 43 percent showed the woman drugged; and 46 percent were billed as incest rape. Fiona Elvines, who works at the rape crisis center, conveyed her personal experience with the porn wars debates. "We work with survivors, and we are seeing the harms of pornography every day in our work and [some academics] say, 'It's not in the research.' But this is practice-based evidence from front-line services.... We are having lots of women talking about being raped and being filmed and that being used as a method for silencing them, but that will take a while to make it into the research papers,"[5] Elvines says.

This urgency without data may be a good strategy in terms of constructing a persuasive point, but it is questionable whether this technique is good science. Journalism professor Robert Jensen also relies on persuasive anti-pornography rhetoric. Jensen goes so far as to expressly dismiss empirical research, writing that he prefers not to be "paralyzed by the limitations of social science," relying instead on his personal testimonials about porn. He is not alone in this approach. On the issue of scientific evidence, philosopher Lori Watson proclaims "no amount of empirical data alone will settle the question as to how best to define and understand pornography." Karen Boyle writes that "it is difficult to imagine how one could be 'objective' about pornography"; and Gail Dines maintains that easily accessible porn "images are all too representative of what is out there on the Internet and in mass-produced movies."[6] Yet according to *Scientific American*, there is no data showing that pornography makes its users more aggressive, and exposure may even make some viewers *less* likely to commit sexual violence. Milton Diamond, director of the Pacific Center for Sex and Society at the University of Hawaii at Manoa, says the porn debate is "a moral issue, not a factual issue"; yet even this statement stands in direct opposition to the point made in Catharine MacKinnon's famous essay, "Not a Moral Issue," in which she argues that pornography is a political matter that distorts sexual reality.

As psychologist Michael Bader writes, "Porn is not harmless. But neither is it an important cause of sexual violence or misogyny. Partisans on both sides of this debate have littered their arguments with distortions, hyperbole, and cheap rhetorical tricks."[7] To paraphrase Bader, we have to wade through a lot of rubbish to get to the truth.

### *Does Pornography Mean that We Are What We Watch?*

Watching pornography evokes questions about the role of curiosity and exploration in shaping and expressing human sexuality. In response to concerns that pornography is sexist and promotes misogyny among its male viewers, University of Montreal professor Simon Louis Lajeunesse reports that his male test subjects say they support gender equality. "Pornography hasn't changed their perception of women or their relationship which they all want as harmonious and fulfilling as possible. Those who could not live out their fantasy in real life with their partner simply set aside the fantasy. The fantasy is broken in the real world and men don't want their partner to look like a porn star," says Lajeunesse.[8] In other words, research shows that people who watch porn are able to tell the difference between fantasy and reality.

Furthermore, sexual fantasy alone is not a good indicator of psychopathology, and in fact, the opposite may be true. Yet, if critics charge that pornography contributes to misogyny, racism, and violence toward women, then this raises an important query: does the kind of porn people view reflect who they are or what they really want in real life? Does enjoying BDSM (Bondage and Discipline; Sadism and Masochism; Dominance and Submission) porn mean the user is violent or wants to be a victim? Or does enjoying gay or lesbian porn mean that the viewer is gay? If gay people watch straight porn, does that mean they're hetero curious? Does enjoying straight porn mean the user is heterosexual? Does sexual arousal over fantasy rape scenes mean the user wants to rape—or to be raped?

"As a feminist," writes Anna Pulley about her experience watching a live porn, "I've found there's often a negotiation that occurs when watching most porn, especially if it involves any kind of heavy aggression or degradation. Because, let's face it, our desires are hardly ever politically correct."[9] A study in the *Journal of Sexual Medicine* found that 30–60 percent of women had fantasies with themes of submission, such as being spanked or tied up and forced to have sex. This was corroborated by a Pornhub survey of male and female viewing patterns that found women were 80–100 percent more likely than men to browse sections like "Rough Sex," "Double Penetration," and "Gangbang." It turns out that women are looking for graphic keywords. "Big dick," "hardcore," and "fisting" are among a few of the search categories that women view more often than men.

But what about pornography's link to violence or degradation toward men? "Cuckold," "femdom," and "sissy" are popular genres that might seem to raise red flags about gender, power, and exploitation. Yet critics tend not to be alarmed about the portrayal of masculinity in pornography, except to emphasize the construction of violent male sexuality.

Researchers from Québec, Canada, find that some sexual fantasies—such as an openly homosexual man who has heterosexual fantasies—might be experienced as upsetting or painful, but there is not evidence they are harmful. And as for fantasies that are considered "unusual"—such as the content in fetish porn—these folks, the researchers say, "may be as sexually satisfied, if not more, than individuals who do not have such fantasies."

As for on-the-job satisfaction? Several former models have filed suit against the BDSM site Kink.com, claiming they were denied workers' compensation for injuries sustained on set, injuries some claim stem from dangers that are inherent to the industry.

### Does Pornography Cause Sexism and Racism?

One study in Copenhagen investigated the links between (a) past exposure to pornography and sexist attitudes and (b) current personality traits and sexist attitudes. Among the women in this study, past pornography use was not associated with having sexist beliefs. In comparison, men's past pornography use was at first found to be linked with negative attitudes toward women including greater hostility, negative prejudices, and stereotypes. However, when participants were exposed to pornography in the laboratory and assessed for core personality traits, another finding emerged. The level of agreeableness was found to influence the relationship between pornography and sexist attitudes. Individuals who are disagreeable have higher levels of antagonism, coldness, hostility, suspiciousness, unfriendliness, and self-interest. Only those who scored low in agreeableness were found to have an increase in sexist attitudes when they were shown pornography. What this means is that viewing pornography can be linked to increased sexism—but not necessarily among all people. In other words, pornography seems to lead to sexism among the men and women who are already unpleasant people.

This study may provide nuance to better understand when, for whom, and under what conditions adverse effects of pornography are most likely. This study also raises important questions about other findings. A study by anti-violence educator John Foubert found that college men in fraternities who watch porn are unlikely to intervene as bystanders to sexual violence, they demonstrate an increased intent to rape, and they are more likely to believe in rape myths (e.g., "she was asking for it"). But the Copenhagen findings raise the issue as to whether the initial problem is porn or personality.

Sexism, although tremendously impactful, is only one of several intersecting issues concerning the politics of pornography. Scholars such as Mireille Miller-Young have studied the relationship between pornography, race, and gender, noting both the problems of racism and the progressive potential in this media genre.

In her book *A Taste for Brown Sugar,* Miller-Young examined representations of black women's sexuality in pornography. She relied heavily on interviews with performers about their personal experience to document the voices of black female sex workers in navigating the complicated history of a complex industry. "Black feminist critics since the late 1970s have largely dismissed pornography as inherently violent and dangerous," wrote Miller-Young. Sociologist Patricia Hill Collins described the condition of black women in pornography as embodying "the existence of victim and pet" who "does not control her body." Alice Walker commented that for centuries, black women "served as the primary pornographic 'outlet' for White men in Europe and America"; and contemporary representations continue that history of racist sexual violence against black women's bodies.

Coexisting with sexist racism is the fact that some black women and men in pornography are "working hard to create their own images, express their own desires, and shape their own labor choices and conditions,"[10] wrote Miller-Young. Adult performer Betty Blac described in an interview with Miller-Young her experience working in the heterosexual market for Big Beautiful Women, which typically fetishizes the bodies of voluptuous women. "There's one director who shall remain nameless," Blac said. "He offered my white friend three scenes but he only offered me one blowjob scene [because] he didn't really feel like black Big Beautiful Women (BBW) were as marketable. He was only willing to work with me because I was light skinned. I sent him an email and said basically, 'You're a racist.'" But that experience is not unique. If you go to the "plumper" websites and take a look at the women who are in the ads and on the splash page, Blac explains, it's easy to see that companies promote white women more.[11]

Adult film performer Janice Griffith seconded Blac's observations about racism in the industry, explaining to *The Independent* that not only are there fewer opportunities for people of color who work in the porn industry, but people of color are pigeonholed, fetishized, and are often paid less compared with white people or those who can pass for white. The Internet only exacerbates the problem.

The Internet keywords that are available when people use a search engine are predetermined by entering various terms that are linked to websites. This system for tagging search terms means that people can find the content that they're looking for, and it means that porn users can target their specific sexual desires. But it also means that entire categories of people and sexual acts are delineated by the language that is available online. Online tags sort content into menus; among these are ethnic or cultural characteristics of the performers including nationality, geographic region, skin color, race, and religion. There are platforms that allow uploaders to select their own indexing words for their videos. This presumably provides greater diversity in descriptions, although it's not clear, given the opportunity, how many porn uploaders use innovative terms for describing people and sexuality and how many simply repeat the existing narrative tropes.

A group of French researchers looked closely at these deep tags and found a pattern of associations. Among the three most frequently tagged nationality categories, certain porn categories were statistically overrepresented: "Japanese" is overly associated with "massage" and "bukkake"; "German" is associated with "Gothic" and "grannies"; and "French" is tied to "Arab," "anal," and "gangbang." The authors of the article "Deep Tags" explain that a video uploaded with keywords indicating nationality does not necessarily take place in the related country. The tags don't necessarily reflect an actor's actual nationality or ethnicity. Nor do tags accurately describe a country's preferred sexual practices. Rather, these tags and keywords are indicators of stereotypes or prejudice.

Whereas gay, transsexual, and bisexual are tagged categories of porn, heterosexual is not. Although Latina, ebony, and
interracial are tagged, white is not. This reveals the implicit
race and sexual bias embedded in pornography vis-à-vis
keywords and tags. Unmarked terms are privileged with the
assumption of being part of a dominant norm. Categories that
are not heterosexual, white, or cisgender are set apart and
defined, thus demarcating sociopolitical privilege and mar-
ginalization. "Tags can have different meanings in different
contexts. Uses of porn categories greatly depend on national
and geographical context. For example, the 'Beurette' (Arab
girl in French) category is not understandable in isolation from
an understanding of the French colonial past and postcolonial
contemporary relationships, which produce young Arab girls
as objects of desire for a white male gaze."[12]

Sinnamon Love, a performer who describes herself as mul-
tiethnic, self-identified African American, says that "racism is
a symptom of the bigger problem of society and porn no more
contributes to that than any other form of commercial media.
Although there is certainly an element of racism in some adult
movies, this is by no means the barometer to judge all pornography. This would be like judging all priests based on a few
child molesters or all Southern white males based on a few
members of the KKK."

It stands to reason that any kind of hate found throughout
society and media is also present in pornography. Although
porn may not cause this hatred, its presence certainly does
not interrupt the pattern. As with so much of pop culture, it
isn't hard to find racism, sexism, and imperialist exploitation.
Yet it also stands to reason that within pornography—as with
all forms of pop culture such as TV, music, or movies—it is
possible to find genres that are nonracist, nonsexist, nontrans-
phobic, and life-affirming. "I'm very critical of the industry's
racial politics and how people of color are treated. But I'm not
anti-porn," says Miller-Young. "Surely there's racism in the
porn industry. It affects how people of color are represented

and treated but there are counter-stories—especially among women of color who are creating and managing their own product. This doesn't get enough attention."

Change is slowly arriving in the world of porn. Some online porn sites are refusing to use traditional porn keyword categories, and more performers are taking creative control by directing their own work. Griffith hopes, as do many others in the field, that as more people of color in the adult industry start to choose their own narratives, the traditional sexist and racist structures in porn will start to break down.

## Are There Links between Pornography and Human Sex Trafficking?

Another important issue points to questions about the labor conditions under which pornography is made and specifically, whether—or to what extent—people appearing in porn videos and photo stills have been sex trafficked.

President and CEO of Morality in Media, Patrick Trueman, writes that pornography leads to a "pandemic of harm," which conditions men to view women as objects for male pleasure and desensitizes men to the pain caused by sexual exploitation. This includes sex trafficking. According to Trueman, pornography "creates the demand for sex trafficking."[13] To his point, because of the easy availability of sex workers, places like Hungary and Thailand are becoming emerging global centers for creating porn. And, although the vast majority of porn websites are hosted in the United States, hosting is also clustered in Russia, Bulgaria, and the Czech Republic where there is worry about coerced labor conditions. *The Economist* reported as early as 1998 that "most West European producers of sex videos use East European actors wherever possible. 'They cost less and do more,' an executive at Germany's Silwa production company explained, bluntly." By 2000, Budapest grew in production size in Europe, "eclipsing rivals such as Amsterdam and Copenhagen." As a result, performers' fees have dropped sharply; and, according to *The Economist*, "even excruciating or humiliating acts usually cost the producer only two or three hundred dollars, roughly a third of the fees paid ten years ago."[14]

These sorts of statements have prompted a growing concern that sex-trafficked women and children from poor countries are being forced into pornography. Anti-sex-trafficking activists and US government figures put the range of global trafficking between 600,000 and 4 million people per year. One CIA report claimed that 700,000 to 2 million women and children are trafficked globally every year. California State Attorney General Kamala Harris told members of the UCLA Law School that 94 percent of trafficked people in California alone are female, and their average age is between 12 and 14 years old. The International Labour Organization estimated in 2014 that of the 18.7 million globally trafficked people, 22 percent are sexually exploited. This transnational organized crime, Harris said, is motivated by money, and the criminals will do whatever they need to earn it. We more easily recognize illegal products trafficked by organized crime such as drugs or counterfeit goods. But human sex trafficking is not visible in the same way. It is especially difficult to track sex trafficking in pornography.

According to the US State Department, human sex trafficking occurs whenever people are made to perform a commercial sex act against their will—either by force, fraud, or coercion—or when any child under the age of 18 is recruited, transported, or harbored for sexual exploitation. It is nearly impossible to determine how many women and children are sex trafficked and even more difficult to know how many sex-trafficked people are specifically forced into pornography. Abolitionist feminists claim that compartmentalizing human trafficking into discrete categories of stripping, sex work, and pornography is pointless. This framework diminishes the harm of sex trafficking, explained activists speaking at UCLA's 2015 Law School Review Symposium. For abolitionists, there is no such

thing as "sex work by choice" or voluntary work in pornography. All forms of sexual labor is human trafficking. Working
in pornography is the "choice" of the choiceless and better
understood as "compensated rape," argue anti-trafficking and
anti-sex work activists such as Autumn Burris, the founder
and director of Survivors for Solutions. Legal scholar and leading anti-trafficking activist Laura Lederer warns, "We should
not say that pornography leads to sex trafficking; pornography
is sex trafficking."[15]

Some caution, however, that abolitionist arguments against
pornography amount to a moral crusade based on human sex-
trafficking figures that are unreliable, false, or exaggerated—
often to make a political point rather than to understand
what is actually happening. Even the CIA report cited previously acknowledges that there is no single agency that is
compiling accurate data. The United Nations, the US General
Accountability Office, and the Justice Department are also
skeptical of the trafficking figures that are tossed around, citing methodological weaknesses in these claims. Nevertheless,
write coauthors Rebecca Sullivan and Alan McKee, "even if
the numbers are overstated for political effect, any number is
too high and the issue of workplace conditions in the global
pornography industry must be addressed."[16]

### What Is the Impact of Pornography on Marriage and Relationships?

A study published in the journal of *Sex and Marital Therapy*
found that partners who watch porn together experience less
distress. Some suggest that porn use can prevent partners
from cheating; but for others, pornography feels like infidelity. The media reports anecdotal comments by people (usually
women) who say they've been coerced into sexual activity that
did not appeal to them as a result of their partners (usually
men) watching porn. Nineteen-year-old "Alaska" tells *Dame
Magazine* that "having sex with men who are avid porn users

feels like I'm being masturbated into. It feels devoid of intimacy." This points to a valuable question: is pornography toxic for relationships?

Author of *The Psychology of Human Sexuality,* Justin Lehmiller, points out that some research indicates an association between porn use and relationship problems. It's not clear, however, that this research is reliable. The media flocked to one popular study suggesting that *Playboy* magazine caused up to 25 percent of all divorces in the 1960s and 1970s. But this research is actually correlational—not causational—in nature. There are plenty of potential reasons to explain why *Playboy's* readership could have increased at the same time as the divorce rate went up. For instance, no-fault divorce laws eased the ability to end marriages without undo burden; or maybe 1960's "free love" ethos and the 1970's "swinger's" era impacted cultural norms and decisions about marriage. "There is simply no definitive evidence that porn *causes* relationship problems all or even most of the time," says Lehmiller. Certainly, there are some relationships in which porn is a problem. But at the same time, there are many relationships in which watching porn is a positive or shared activity. As Lehmiller puts it, the impact that pornography has on couples "all depends upon the people involved and how they have negotiated their relationship."[17]

In what may seem like science confirming common sense, the main variable in the impact of pornography on relationships turns out to be honesty. Research finds that partners who are honest about the porn they watch have lower levels of relationship distress and higher levels of relationship satisfaction.

### Does Pornography Have Positive Benefits?

Feminist author Naomi Wolf claims that porn is ruining sex and driving men crazy. British couples are having 20 percent less sex every month than they did 10 years ago, and rather than attribute this decline to things such as Netflix or tweeting in bed, Wolf blames pornography. Wolf also comments on the proliferation of high-profile men caught up in sex scandals involving prostitution, sexting, or indiscreet social media. Driving what she calls "weirdly disinhibited decision-making" could be the widespread availability of pornography. Increased porn consumption "could actually be rewiring the male brain, affecting men's judgment about sex and causing them to have more difficulty controlling their impulses," Wolf conjectures in an *Aljazeera* opinion piece titled "Is Pornography Driving Men Crazy?"

Wolf is not alone in her views. But as feminist pornography scholar Constance Penley points out, history provides a wealth of examples of how pornography was used "to challenge absolutist political authority and church doctrine." Porn has been linked to "avant-garde revolutionary art, populist struggles, [and] countercultural impulses."[18] In addition to its free speech aspect, pornography obviously centers on sex. And, counter to the panic over morality issues or the concerns about public safety, there is evidence that using pornography can be an aspect of healthy sexuality.

One Swedish survey found that women between the ages of 35 and 49 had significantly more experience with online pornography than their male cohort. A second Swedish study found that 65 percent of women felt "positive" or "excited" after watching porn. Their enthusiastic feedback included comments about how porn provides tips on new sexual positions, "makes me feel more sexy," and "can wake up the lust." Less than one-third of the women surveyed felt negative toward pornography after using it, and fewer than 10 percent said they felt nothing at all. In Canada, nearly 85 percent of college women surveyed had seen *Playboy* or other "top-shelf" magazines, and two-thirds said porn positively affected their sexual behavior.

Responding to a survey conducted by PornResearch.org about the effects of porn use, one person replied, "It helps me to express the sexual part of my identity. Since menopause I've found that my sexual responsiveness has decreased, although my desire has not. Using porn helps me." Another respondent said, "My partner and I are in a long-distance relationship. We send links of porn to each other as a way of keeping things fresh and hot." And a third person responded that pornography "helped to clarify what excited me."[19]

Not only is the assumption of male victimizer/female victim far more complicated than an exclusively harm-based perspective, there is compelling evidence that *some* pornography can be liberating and empowering, not to mention entertaining and pleasurable to large segments of every society investigated.

Writing for the *American Journal of Sexuality Education,* researchers Mary Ann Watson and Randyl D. Smith conclude that in addition to sexual pleasure, there may also be positive uses of pornography in educational, medical, and clinical settings. Pornography can be used by psychologists, sex therapists, and physicians to jump-start patient's arousal or to decrease shyness. Porn can provide examples of loving sexuality for those who have been sexually abused and can be used to support active sex lives following cardiac surgery or spinal cord injury. The sheer volume and variety of pornographic materials have led to heightened concern about the damaging effects of pornography on society. It is unfortunate, say Watson and Smith, that anti-pornography rhetoric and moral panic may create a hostile climate that undermines the potential value of some sexually explicit material in certain settings.

# 7

# LEGAL ISSUES

## *Why Does the First Amendment Protect Pornography as Free Speech?*

The right to free speech is fundamental to a truly democratic society. Free speech, guaranteed by law, enables people to express themselves, debate ideas, and to search for truth. Without these rights, democratic self-governance is impossible, and creative expression becomes bleak. But what should be done about forms of expression that offend us? Should the right to create, sell, or enjoy sexually graphic images and stories be protected? What if that sexually explicit material seems to cross a line from titillating to obscene? Does the US Constitution suggest that we just have to put up with affronts to one's sensibilities and sexual morality in the name of free speech?

Given that free speech is crucial in promoting all other democratic rights, jurisprudence holds that the government may limit the right to express ourselves only in the most compelling situations. The free-speech guarantee established by the First Amendment is intentionally designed to protect the rights of even small, unpopular minority views against any political tyranny by the majority or by those in power.

Free speech issues fall into two general categories: those that are considered content-neutral cases and those that are content based. Content-neutral cases revolve around the manner or scope of distribution. An example might be a city ban against passing out pamphlets outside grocery stores to prevent littering. These content-neutral cases are subject to what is called intermediate scrutiny, meaning that any law or regulation banning such speech must serve an important government interest.

If a law regulates speech on the basis of its content, this regulation must be examined using the far more stringent standard of strict scrutiny. First Amendment attorney Kimberly Harchuck explains that to pass strict scrutiny, government action to restrict content-based speech must serve a compelling government interest and be narrowly tailored to achieve that particular interest. In practice, the government rarely censors or takes recourse against speech in this context, but it can.

### What Makes Pornography Different from Obscenity?

Although the US Constitution's First Amendment is the foundation of democratic engagement, not all forms of expression are automatically protected. In regard to sexually explicit material, the courts have ruled that although pornography is legal, the states may rule that obscenity is not. There is a long and important history of legal cases in the United States that address the distinction between the two.

The case of *Roth v. United States* (1957) involved Samuel Roth, a New York City vendor who was convicted of violating federal obscenity law. Samuel Roth ran a literary business in New York. He was convicted under a federal statute that criminalized sending "obscene, lewd, lascivious or filthy" materials through the mail for advertising. Roth was also convicted for selling a publication called *American Aphrodite* ("A Quarterly for the Fancy-Free"). *American Aphrodite* contained literary erotica and nude photography.

The Supreme Court upheld Roth's conviction; but rather than using previous obscenity standards banning material that could "deprave and corrupt those whose minds are open to such immoral influences," the *Roth* decision now determined that obscenity referred to material that is "utterly without redeeming value." The question, of course, was how do the courts decide what has redeeming value and what does not?

To answer this question of whether the publications in this case had redeeming value, the Court established the Roth Test. This would come to be applied to future obscenity questions on a case-by-case basis. Based on Roth, material could be banned as obscene if the "average person, applying contemporary community standards" would find that the "dominant theme taken as a whole appeals to the prurient interest." Writing for the Court, Justice William Brennan simply and directly stated that the First Amendment does not protect obscenity.

The Roth Test remained in place as the standard for deciding obscenity cases until *Miller v. California* (1973) and *Pope v. Illinois* (1987). In *Miller*, the court famously replaced the Roth Test by establishing new standards to determine whether material is obscene. The details of the case are as follows.

Marvin Miller was an owner/operator of a California mail-order business that specialized in pornographic films and books. In 1971, Miller sent out a brochure advertising four books and a film that graphically depicted sexual activity between men and women. Five of these brochures were mailed to a restaurant in Newport Beach. The restaurant owner and his mother opened the envelope, saw the brochures, and called the police.

Miller was arrested and charged with violating the California Penal Code, which states (in part) that a person who knowingly sends, sells, possesses, publishes, produces, or shows other people any obscene matter is, for a first offense, guilty of a misdemeanor. The question before the Court was whether selling and distributing obscene material was protected under the First Amendment's guarantee of freedom of speech.

The Court ruled again that the First Amendment did not protect selling and distributing obscene material. However, the Court also acknowledged "the inherent dangers of undertaking to regulate any form of expression." Because the right to free speech is fundamental to democracy and a free society, however, "statutes that regulate obscene materials must be carefully limited." To better uphold the law while carefully weighing the issues, the US Supreme Court created a new, three-part test to determine whether material is obscene.

According to the Miller Test, the First Amendment does not protect material first, if an average person, applying contemporary community standards, would find that the work, taken as a whole, appeals to "the prurient interest"; second, if the work depicts or describes, in a patently offensive way, sexual conduct or excretory functions specifically defined by applicable state law; and third, if the work, taken as a whole, lacks serious literary, artistic, political, or scientific value. The Supreme Court explained that questionable material may not be considered obscene unless it satisfies all three aspects of the Miller Test.

One important aspect of *Miller* was that it drilled down on the geographic aspect of the contemporary community standards against which obscenity was to be measured. Prior to *Miller*, many questioned whether "community standards" about obscenity were based on national or local community standards. The Supreme Court explained in deciding *Miller* that standards for both prurient interest and patent offensiveness could not be constitutionally measured at a national level. A second important issue that resulted from *Miller* was the shift from questioning whether material was *utterly* without social value to determining if this material lacked *serious* value. The distinction between the two concepts may seem like a minor tweak in the language; but this change "created a much lower threshold for unprotected speech, thus resulting in an expanded scope of obscenity and, ultimately, subjecting much more expression to government regulation."[1]

Still, it remained unclear, based on *Miller*, how to assess whether a work lacked *serious* literary, artistic, political, or scientific value. In 1987, *Pope v. Illinois* modified this third prong of the Miller Test.

In *Pope*, a detective from the local police department entered a Rockford, Illinois, adult bookstore store in July 1983 and purchased three magazines: *Anal Animal, Full Throttle,* and *Fuck Around*. Richard Pope, a clerk at the adult bookstore, was arrested for violating an Illinois state criminal statute prohibiting the sale of obscene magazines. A jury convicted Richard Pope of violating this law.

At Pope's trial, the judge instructed the jury to determine the value of the magazines based on how they thought "ordinary adults in the State of Illinois" (i.e., a form of community standard) would view them. The jury found Pope guilty, and the judge fined him $3,000 and sentenced him to nearly a year in prison.

Pope appealed his case to the US Supreme Court, where his lawyers argued that this conviction should be overturned because the Illinois court improperly relied on the community standard in finding the magazines Pope sold lacked "social value." The Supreme Court agreed, ruling that the idea of a community standard was inappropriate for determining whether a work had value.

The Supreme Court vacated Pope's conviction. (The Court also remanded the case to the State Appellate Court to reconsider related issues in the matter.) Specifically, the Court held that the proper question is not whether an *ordinary* member of any given community would find serious literary, artistic, political, or scientific value in allegedly obscene material but whether a *reasonable* person would find such value in the material, taken as a whole. This kind of value, wrote Justice White, does not vary from community to community according to whether or to what degree the public accepts the work. Justice White concluded that contrary to the approach taken in Illinois, proper inquiry did not rely on how ordinary members of a particular community view the social value of an allegedly obscene work; rather, appropriate inquiry depends on whether a reasonable person, using by implication a national standard, found social value in the work taken as a whole. Justice White stressed that the majority opinion in *Miller* was careful to point out that the First Amendment protects works of serious value "regardless of whether the government or a majority of the people approve of the ideas these works represent."

In sum, although *Pope v. Illinois* modified the third prong of the Miller Test to apply the standards of a reasonable (rather than ordinary) person, Justice Scalia and Justice Stevens point out in their concurring and dissenting opinions that the reasonable person standard still leaves defendants at the whim of juries that account for their own personal taste in assessing what a reasonable person would find valuable.

Some argue that this debate over whether legal standards ought to rely on ordinary or reasonable people misses the point entirely. Feminist legal theorist Catharine MacKinnon argues that the whole concept of both ordinary people *and* reasonable people presumes this generic person is male. At the heart of the matter, MacKinnon says, the issue is not whether pornography is obscene but that it harms women.

As MacKinnon sees it, the entire standard for determining obscenity is built on what the male standpoint sees; and in pornography, "women desire dispossession and cruelty. Men, permitted to put words (and other things) in women's mouths, create scenes in which women desperately want to be bound, battered, tortured, humiliated, and killed. Or merely taken and used. This is erotic to the male point of view." Pornography is not simply representation or imagery. It is not expression or fantasy, MacKinnon writes. "It is sexual reality." And thus, argues MacKinnon, the courts' concern with obscenity is misguided because pornography is already the harm. Whereas obscenity discourse centers on whether sexually explicit material is morally decent, focusing on harm instead shifts the focus to matters of sexual equality and sexual violence.

In her essay "Not a Moral Issue," MacKinnon writes that "pornography does not work sexually without hierarchy. If there is no inequality, no violation, no dominance, no force, there is no sexual arousal." And, furthermore, this model of sexualized inequality, she says, extends into all facets of everyday life, relegating women to second-class status. Based on this perspective, MacKinnon, working with activist Andrea Dworkin, drafted model legislation for the cities of Indianapolis and Minneapolis. These ordinances used a civil rights foundation to attack pornography, arguing that pornography is sex discrimination: it eroticizes domination and inequality and "makes sexism sexy." The ordinances defined pornography as the graphic sexually explicit subordination of women through pictures or in words.

Instead of relying on criminal penalties and obscenity charges, the Antipornography Civil Rights Ordinances authorized women harmed by pornography to file civil lawsuits and seek damages in the case of four offenses: trafficking in pornography, coercion into pornography, forcing pornography on a person, and assault or physical attack due to pornography. In defining pornography, the ordinance also stipulated that the subordinating words or pictures include one of the following nine conditions:[2]

1. women are presented as dehumanized sexual objects, things, or commodities; or
2. as sexual objects who enjoy pain or humiliation; or
3. as sexual objects who experience sexual pleasure in being raped; or
4. as sexual objects that are tied, cut up, mutilated, bruised, or physically hurt; or
5. in postures of sexual submission; or
6. women's body parts—including but not limited to vaginas, breasts, or buttocks—are exhibited such that women are reduced to those parts; or
7. women are presented as whores by nature; or
8. being penetrated by objects or animals; or
9. women are presented in scenarios of degradation, injury, abasement, torture, shown as filthy or inferior, bleeding, bruised, or hurt in a context that makes these conditions sexual.

The anti-pornography ordinance also stated that "The use of men, children, or transsexuals [sic] in the place of women in this definition is also pornography for purposes of this law."

First passed in 1983, in Minneapolis, the same law was passed in Indianapolis one year later. The Indianapolis version omitted from its definition of pornography the preceding first, fifth, and seventh sections.

In an ironic political dovetailing of the radical left and the reactionary right, the ordinance passed with the support of conservative politicians who consistently opposed women's rights issues. Catharine MacKinnon and Andrea Dworkin are considered radical feminists, yet every Democratic member of the Indianapolis city council voted against this ordinance, and every Republican member voted in favor of it.[3] Not one local feminist organization supported the law, and the local chapter of the National Organization for Women (NOW) opposed it.

Although the Minneapolis City Council adopted the anti-pornography ordinance twice in 1983, the city's mayor vetoed it on the grounds that it violated the First Amendment. In Indianapolis, Mayor William Hudnut, both a conservative Republican and a minister, signed the anti-pornography bill into law. Less than two hours later, a coalition of booksellers and publishers filed suit in federal court opposing the new law. In deciding the resulting case, *American Booksellers Association v. Hudnut* (1985), the Federal Trial Court and the Federal Court of Appeals struck down the Indianapolis ordinance as a violation of the First Amendment. The US Supreme Court affirmed this ruling.

In line with the Supreme Court's decision, former ACLU president Nadine Strossen argues in her book *Defending Pornography* that feminist anti-pornography efforts are not fundamentally about harm against women. To start, MacKinnon and Dworkin's definition of pornography is "hopelessly vague." Efforts to censor pornography are, in Strossen's view (and for many others), a fundamental violation of free speech rights. Moreover, these anti-pornography efforts undermine women's equality by insisting that the law treat women in a special and particular way. In the words of Judge Frank Easterbrook, who sat on the Seventh Circuit Court that decided *Hudnut* on initial appeal, regardless of one's opinion about pornography that depicts women as sexually submissive or humiliated, "the Constitution forbids the government to declare one perspective right and silence opponents."

Yet despite Easterbrook's point, government opinions about pornography have differed wildly. A commission under President Nixon determined that consensual adult pornography had no measurable bad effects. The 1986 Report of the Meese Pornography Commission, established by former president Ronald Reagan, detailed the allegedly harmful effects of pornography. The Meese Commission led to sweeping attacks on works including the illustration-filled manual *The Joy of Sex*—yet the Meese report was also criticized as biased and inaccurate. Some joked that the report itself was pornographic. Sexpert Susie Bright claimed she "came three times" while reading it.

During Republican George W. Bush's presidential administration, Justice Department data shows that prosecutors brought obscenity charges against 361 defendants. This was almost twice as many charges compared with the number filed under Democratic President Bill Clinton. During the first year of Barack Obama's presidency, twenty defendants were charged, compared with fifty-four obscenity charges during the previous year.

### What Are Some Important Legal Cases Regarding Pornography in the United States?

Despite the long history of legal and political debate on the topic, crucial questions continue to face the courts and the court of public opinion: Where do we draw the line between pornography and obscenity, between free speech, pleasure, and harm? And who decides?

Significant legal cases have also addressed whether pornography is prostitution, if compensation may be awarded in cases of intentional emotional harm, when or how interstate commerce laws impact distribution, and matters of child pornography as criminal violations of the law. The following cases provide a brief overview of these key issues.

In *California v. Freeman* (1989), the California State Supreme Court ruled that filming sexual activity was not the same thing as criminal pandering or prostitution. The ruling thus established that it was legal to produce adult film in California. Since this decision, Los Angeles County has emerged as a worldwide center for the adult film industry; and as of 2005, an estimated 80 percent of all production took place in Los Angeles County. Despite the size of the adult industry, questions persist about whether certain kinds of pornography should be against the law.

In *Hustler Magazine, Inc. v. Falwell* (1988), the US Supreme Court unanimously ruled that the First Amendment free speech guarantee prohibits awarding damages to public figures as compensation for intentional emotional harm. The case was generated from a lampooning of televangelist pastor and founder of the Moral Majority Jerry Falwell. *Hustler*'s parody riffed on an actual ad campaign for Campari that featured famous people describing their "first time."

The Campari ad campaign used this double entendre as a reference to both sex and to drinking the liqueur. In the Falwell case, *Hustler* created a fake ad featuring a fictional interview with Falwell talking about his "first time" with his mother. The spoof includes the fake Falwell saying that they were so "drunk off their asses" on Campari that "Mom looked better than a Baptist whore with a $100 donation." Since his "mother" had shown "all the other guys in town such a good time," he figured "What the hell."

The magazine included small print explaining the fake ad was "parody—not to be taken seriously"—but Falwell sued and was initially awarded $150,000 for intentional infliction of emotional distress. On appeal, the Court found that reasonable people would understand that the advertisement was a joke, not a true story, and deemed the ad was political satire. The Court explained this case went beyond the question of emotional distress to the issue of First Amendment free speech. Falwell argued that the *Hustler* parody was so outrageous that it went beyond free speech. "The fact that society may find speech offensive is [however] not a reason for suppressing it," wrote Chief Justice William Rehnquist.

In other areas of the law, the intent to inflict harm is not a protected right; but in regard to free speech, once again, the importance of robust exchange of opinion and the free flow of ideas took priority over outrage. The Jerry Falwell case provided the storyline for the popular 1996 mainstream movie, *The People vs. Larry Flynt*, starring Woody Harrelson, Edward Norton, and Courtney Love. Based on this story and others, Larry Flynt became what Erin Moriarty of the CBS news show "48 Hours" described as "an unlikely champion of the Constitution."

About a decade later, the Bush administration launched its War on Porn, forming the Obscenity Prosecution Task Force. Under the Department of Justice, this task force was dedicated to pursuing obscenity prosecutions. In 2005, the FBI began recruiting agents for its Adult Obscenity Squad to gather evidence against "manufacturers and purveyors" of adult pornography (and the "porn squad" became a source of many jokes among FBI employees).

Two infamous cases that emerged from these task force efforts involved high-profile pornographers and resulted in vastly different outcomes. In the first case, John "Buttman" Stagliano was indicted by a federal grand jury in Washington, DC, on federal obscenity charges. Stagliano, and his company Evil Angel, was charged with seven felony counts of selling obscene material through the Internet. The indictment specifically cited Jay Sin's *Milk Nymphos*, Joey Silvera's *Storm Squirters 2*, and an online trailer for Belladonna's *Fetish Fanatic 5*.

In *Miller* and *Pope,* the courts had established that the "community" determines what sorts of material are obscene. It was no accident that the charges were filed in the District of Columbia, where, presumably, local sentiment would be more publically conservative than in Los Angeles. However, *Miller* and *Pope* still left open the question of who comprises the Internet community. A tongue-in-cheek headline in *Wired* magazine described the case, declaring "Feds Charge Porn Producer With Selling Adult Content to Adults."

The judge agreed with the sentiment of the *Wired* headline and dismissed the charges with reprimand toward the government. The case had been riddled with technical glitches and a questionable FBI witness, or what the *Washington City Paper* called "a series of fuck-ups by the United States Government." Chastising the prosecution, US District Court Judge Richard J. Leon said the evidence presented by the Justice Department's Obscenity Prosecution Task Force was "woefully insufficient" and that hopefully the government would "learn a lesson from its experience."

At about this same time, pornographer Paul F. Little was found guilty of distributing obscene material over the Internet and through the US mail. In this case, the defendant (aka Max Hardcore) was found guilty of twenty counts of obscenity and sentenced to nearly four years in federal prison. Although there were journalists who heralded this case as yet another free speech issue among consenting adults, *Forbes* author Susannah Breslin staunchly disagreed with this assessment, writing that Max Hardcore's extreme pornography included unprecedented degradation. The women of these films, Breslin wrote, "are choked, slapped, throat-fucked, penetrated with fists, given enemas, pile-driven, urinated upon, vomited upon, and in some instances instructed to drink from glasses the money shots that have been delivered into their rectums."[4] His pornography is so extreme that Max Hardcore is considered a victimizer and a pariah within his own industry. "He's rumored to have put several actresses in the hospital, and most starlets refuse to work with him; porn queen Nici Sterling calls him a 'psychopath,'" writes Peter Scholtes for the Minneapolis *City Pages*. Scenes in Max Hardcore's videos are often "fraught with pedophilia themes, beginning when he stumbles upon his subjects in playgrounds, where they sit alone, in pigtails, talking baby-talk, and sucking on lolli-pops,"[5] writes Breslin. This theme initially resulted in 1998 child pornography charges against Max Hardcore for content representing children under the age of 18. However, before the case was brought to trial, the Supreme Court ruling in *Ashcroft v. Free Speech Coalition* (2002) established that it was unconstitutional to prohibit adults from portraying children in films and books. Based on this ruling, the child pornography charges were dismissed.

This constitutional limitation on punishing *representations* of minors notwithstanding, actual child pornography is a crime. In their book on media studies, Alan McKee and Rebecca Sullivan explain that the preferred language for this criminal material is *child abuse materials* rather than what some call "child pornography." The First Amendment does not protect child abuse materials, nor is it tolerated in other nations around the world. In Britain, a 2014 dragnet resulted in the arrest of more than 600 suspected pedophiles accused with accessing pornographic images of children online.

In *New York v. Ferber* (1982), the Court ruled that the government could lawfully restrict distribution of child pornography to protect children from the harm inherent in making it. In *Osborne v. Ohio* (1990), this ruling was extended to apply to possession of child pornography, again to protect children from harm. The Child Online Protection Act—or COPA—enacted in 1998, was intended to impose penalties on American porn websites that allowed minors to access harmful material. In *Ashcroft v. American Civil Liberties Union* (2002), the US Supreme Court overturned the law on the grounds that it would infringe on free speech for adults. The Court's opinion stated that filtering programs were adequate for preventing underage access to adult material. Known simply as "2257," the colloquial term refers to federal law that protects children from exploitation. The law requires that all porn performers provide evidence that they are over eighteen and requires detailed record keeping by porn producers in this regard. Intended to prevent child sexual abuse, 2257 has also had a chilling effect on sex educators and erotic photographers who are hindered by—or simply not able to provide—the time-consuming paperwork required under the current iteration of the law.

### What Is Measure B?

In 2012, voters passed an ordinance mandating condom use by porn performers during filming throughout Los Angeles County. Measure B was supported by AIDS activists and backed by the AIDS Healthcare Foundation (AHF). Arguments in support of Measure B emphasized that mandatory condom use would prevent disease and infectious outbreaks among porn performers and would prevent transmission among their nonindustry sex partners. Critics counter that Measure B is a censorship issue pitting the power of the state against individual freedoms. (I discuss additional details about the medical aspects of mandatory condom laws in chapter 8.)

Porn industry advocates, such as the Free Speech Coalition, fought Measure B, arguing, in part, that mandatory condom use violates the First Amendment right to free expression. Furthermore, the group points out, routine testing already required by the porn industry is an effective measure in preventing HIV and sexually transmitted infections. Additionally, the State of California's Division of Occupational Safety and Health (Cal/OSHA) is already available to receive any pertinent complaints and to enforce safety standards that protect workers from health hazards on the job.

When it comes to mandating condom use, however, industry insiders argue that there is little market demand for seeing porn that includes condoms. Measure B, they explain, is actually an attempt to push the porn industry out of business. Many performers object to mandatory condoms for health reasons of their own. Sex that is performed for porn videos takes a lot longer than everyday (non-porn) sex. The friction caused by condoms causes discomfort and possible abrasions, which paradoxically puts performers at a higher risk of infection. Supporters of Measure B claim the porn industry puts profit before safety when they insist that sex scenes with condoms don't sell.

A few production companies, such as Wicked Pictures, voluntarily require condom use in their shoots. Wicked also opposes Measure B. In 2013, companies such as Vivid Entertainment sued Los Angeles County to prevent implementation of Measure B. Regardless of the law, condoms are routinely avoided in porn shoots. This prompted AHF to file Cal/OSHA complaints against nearly twenty gay and straight productions between 2009 and 2014, including Hustler, Vivid, Reality Kings, and Bang Bros. One argument frequently suggested by the adult industry in avoiding mandatory condom use is that performers are independent contractors and are therefore not covered by workplace law. In 2014, a California judge ruled that porn performers in California should be treated as employees and are therefore covered by California workplace laws requiring condoms.

On January 30, 2014, Assembly Bill 1576 was introduced into the California State Legislature. This proposed measure would have mandated statewide requirements to use condoms in adult films; and, under certain circumstances, violation of the act would be a crime. The bill was shelved in the State Senate Appropriations Committee that same year, but the AHF, which sponsored the bill, promised to reintroduce the controversial legislation. Although Measure B and mandatory condom policies are county- and state-based measures, there are global implications in terms of health, workplace safety, and freedom of expression.

### What Are Some of the Global Pornography Laws?

The adult industry routinely faces censorship and legal challenges around the globe. For instance, in 1984, the British Board of Film Classification (BBFC) was tasked with broader regulatory powers including the ability to block a film release entirely. Although these policy changes were initially designed to address horror films, one of the BBFC's first actions was to ban the release of all hard-core porn videos and DVDs. This ban lasted until 2000 when distributors and retailers won a legal challenge. Beyond this ruling, however, the adult industry in the United Kingdom has shown little interest in collectively opposing censorship. In the past, the adult industry was somewhat protected in Britain. Soft-core titles sold with little restriction; imported hard-core DVDs required BBFC certification and could only be sold in licensed sex shops, which numbered less than 400. The Internet changed all this.

When the British Parliament voted in favor of opt-in Internet filtering, the industry barely objected. Nor has the industry vocally opposed the argument to ban entire URLs. One reason is because there's been hope on the part of the adult industry that limited access to online porn might help boost flagging DVD sales. Secondly, the BBFC and other similar regulators are unelected bodies wielding tremendous power. Without First Amendment free speech protections, the adult industry is reticent about resisting censorship efforts.[6] Furthermore, by 2014, legal changes in Britain further meant that pay-to-play video-on-demand must conform to the Audiovisual Media Services Regulations and content must be classified in accordance with the R18 guidelines established by the BBFC. In effect this means that content providers may no longer offer online pornography that couldn't also be bought in a sex shop. Intended to prevent distribution of content that could incite hatred or impair children, acts that may no longer be shown include spanking (beyond a gentle level), penetration by any object associated with violence, and activities that could be life endangering such as face-sitting. According to *Vice*, also prohibited are physical or verbal abuse, even if consensual; the portrayal of rape; "water sports"; and female ejaculation.[7] Opponents point out that many of the legally forbidden acts appear to be arbitrarily chosen (water sports), of dubious danger risk (face-sitting), or to highlight women's sexual pleasure (female ejaculation).

A sample of other legislation from around the world includes Uganda's laws banning child pornography. This same law also prohibits erotic music and miniskirts above the knee. In 2014, Japan's Parliament finally banned possession of child pornography after years of international pressure to resolve their lax laws that endangered children. The law does not, however, ban explicit depictions of children in Manga and Anime. Japan also requires that all pubic hair and genitals be censored in pornography. And the Australian Classification Board (ACB), which classifies all adult films before they can be made available to the public, bans pornography that features small-breasted women because they look young. The ACB made this decision to counter pedophilia and child pornography using a legal clause that prohibits images of those younger than 18 and those who appear to be. At this time, the Australian organization also prohibited depictions of women ejaculating during orgasm.

The International Age Rating Coalition (IARC) is a global program that attempts to classify content to provide age-based ratings for various regions based on their local laws and customs. The system targets digital games and online apps; but what this also means is that material such as dictionaries that depict human anatomy, use sexual slang, or include the word "pornography" are labeled as unsuitable for children. The goal is to provide a tool for parents to more easily decide whether content is unsuitable for children. To date, the IARC has been adopted by Google Play and by the United Kingdom, the United States, Canada, Brazil, and most of Europe.

In 2013, the European Union proposed a ban on pornography across all platforms, including the Internet. The goal was to eradicate negative gender stereotypes. The robust debate ended with the European Parliament rejecting the proposal in 2015. (The EU's net neutrality decision made this same year further determined that mandatory porn filters are illegal; Britain's Prime Minister David Cameron defended Internet filters and vowed that the government would find a way around the law.)

Iceland has also proposed a ban on pornography. Minister of the Interior Ogmundur Jonasson wrote that the ban, which would include Internet filters to block all online porn, would prevent harm to children and women. In opposition, the International Modern Media Institute wrote that such a ban is an affront to the freedom of expression and information and the basic principles of society. This would not be the first ban, however. Around the world, law enforcement and government agencies monitor for child pornography and other illegal material. Iran, China, and North Korea have some measure of national-level control over the Internet.

Recently, laws against revenge porn—or nonconsensual pornography—have also become a matter of global concern. So-called revenge porn is a form of online harassment that involves people (usually an ex-partner) non-consensually posting nude and otherwise explicit photos in the Internet. The vast majority of perpetrators are men, and the victims are women, although men are sometimes targeted too.

At the time of her tenure as California State Attorney General, Kamala Harris stated her objection to the term "revenge porn." The word *revenge*, she remarked, implies there is a valid reason to lash out. "And *porn* suggests the victim intended [the images] would be distributed publicly. Those terms also invite judgment about the morals of the women, when, in fact, they're victims."[8] These bullying posts are often accompanied by full doxxing of people's names, home addresses, and workplace information. People who post revenge porn inflict trauma on their victims, some of whom have lost jobs, had to change their legal names, and even committed suicide.

In the first US case of its kind, Kevin Bollaert was sentenced in Spring 2015 to eighteen years in prison. Bollaert was convicted of posting more than 10,000 revenge porn images and then demanding up to $350 from victims to remove these sexually explicit photos. As of 2015, sixteen US states had active laws addressing revenge porn (up from just three states in 2012). New Zealand, Canada, Japan, Australia, and Israel have also addressed revenge porn or cyberbullying as a crime. The challenge, though, is that many laws target repeated actions or direct physical threat. As *The Economist* explains, copyright law cannot help if the victim is the same person who took the photo, and there is evidence that selfies comprise a large percentage of revenge porn. Even if the law can be successfully deployed, it takes a long time to remove the criminal images. And, the Internet being what it is, screen grabs are easy to get and can be reposted elsewhere.

As a solution, Google announced plans to remove revenge porn from its search results. In concert with growing awareness of the problem, the popular social media forums Reddit and Twitter have banned revenge porn from their sites—or at least they have tried.

# 8

# MEDICAL ISSUES

### *Are Porn Performers at Risk of Contracting STIs or HIV?*

In any job, there is a risk of injury or health impact. In highly physical jobs, this danger can be higher. Whenever there is exposure to body fluids, there is a possibility of exposure to an STI and, in some cases, to HIV. There is often cause for attention to this risk among adult performers given that the work can involve both highly physical demands and exposure to ejaculate and mucus. There is debate, however, about whether adult actors are at higher jeopardy than "civilians" outside the porn industry.

Members of the adult film industry consistently claim that as a result of testing and awareness, the rate of STI transmission among performers is lower than the general population. Members of the adult film industry point out that porn performers are routinely tested while other sexually active adults are not. Of concern, they argue, are porn performers who engage in sex with those outside the industry given that civilians are less likely to be frequently tested. The advocacy group FAIR—For Adult Industry Responsibility—points to data indicating, however, that STI transmission rates in the adult film industry are significantly higher compared to the general population. Dr. Robert Kim-Farley says that frequent testing does not guarantee that adult performers are free from HIV or STIs, and it is a myth to say that the adult industry is safer than the general population. In a 2012 study conducted by the Los Angeles County Department of Public

Health, the Johns Hopkins Bloomberg School of Public Health, and UCLA, experts found that 28 percent of adult performers tested positive for chlamydia and/or gonorrhea. In a 2011 study published by the *Journal of Sexually Transmitted Diseases*, performers were found to be 34 times more at risk for chlamydia and 64 times more at risk for gonorrhea than the general Los Angeles County population. This same study found that female performers were 27 percent more likely to have a repeat infection within one year; and it was discovered that about one-third of the porn actors participating in the research project had a previously undiagnosed STI. A second study published in 2012 by the same journal found that 47 of the 168 research participants—all of whom worked in the adult film industry—had at least one sexually transmitted disease. The STI most often present was gonorrhea, contracted through oral or rectal sex. Eighteen of the women in the study had simultaneous oral, anal, and vaginal infections.

These findings contradict arguments that regular testing by porn performers results in disease rates that are no higher than the general population. Out of the forty-seven men and women found to have chlamydia and/or gonorrhea in this particular study, eleven cases would not have been caught using the industry's testing protocol in place at that time. The researchers cautioned that their study probably further underestimated the actual rate of infection for two reasons. First, this could be true because they did not test for chlamydia in the oropharynx and second because they were unable to gain consent for rectal testing among the male porn performers. The authors hypothesize that undiagnosed STIs may be common in the adult film industry because performers frequently engage in unprotected oral and anal intercourse; STIs are often asymptomatic; and because, as of the time this research was conducted, the adult industry relied on urine-based testing protocol.

Between 2004 and 2008, eight people who claimed they were employed in the adult film industry tested positive for

HIV, sparking public concern and debate about health and safety. Under questioning during a Cal/OSHA meeting, the Los Angeles County Department of Public Health (LACDPH) revealed that only four of the eight people were *proven to be active* in the industry at the time of infection; the remaining four claimed they were employed in the adult film industry but may have been testing to *begin* working in porn. According to the LACDPH, this uncertainty points to the need for condom use and, furthermore, that these kinds of figures are only minimum estimates. Except for healthcare workers, reporting one's occupation during testing is not required on the HIV testing report form.

Whereas some point to this situation with alarm, others caution that if we are concerned about HIV and STI transmission, it is important to think rationally and keep things in perspective. During a 2010 public hearing on the issue, Nina Hartley, a longtime veteran of adult film, commented on the eight cases of HIV in the adult industry since 2004. Hartley observed that this rate is low compared to the approximately 100 to 125 new case reports of HIV per month in Los Angeles County. LACDPH representative Peter Kerndt's response to Hartley was that instead of comparing porn performers with the general public, it is fairer to compare the adult industry with nurses—or to other occupational groups in a legal industry who contracted HIV in the course of employment—during the same time period. That number, Kerndt noted, is zero.

Some industry sources claim, however, that there has been no transmission of HIV on porn sets since the now-defunct Adult Industry Media (AIM) implemented testing standards in 2004. On March 13, 2013, Free Speech Coalition CEO Diane Duke issued the following statement: "There hasn't been an on set transmission of HIV since 2004—nationwide. Adult film industry protocols are highly effective."[1] Yet six months later, four porn performers again tested positive for HIV, resulting in a moratorium on filming. Cameron Bay, one of the adult film actors who contracted HIV, said she was naive to trust industry STI tests and said other performers told her not to ask for condoms. Bay urged more porn producers to encourage safer sex on set. "I learned that there's always someone younger and sexier, willing to do something you're not ... I think we need more choices because of that. Condoms should be a choice."[2]

Responding to the crisis, the Free Speech Coalition revealed that the 2013 infections traced back to film shoots that occurred in Nevada where testing is less stringent than in Southern California. The HIV test used for adult performers in Nevada did not detect the virus as early as the rigorous testing protocol recommended by the adult industry. The FSC takes this case as evidence that voluntary testing practice—consistent with industry standards—is crucial in preventing STI and HIV transmission. In contrast, Michael Weinstein, president of the AHF, takes this case as evidence that infections will continue to occur during porn productions, regardless of whether performers are tested. As one result of the 2013 HIV alert, producer Tristan Taormino (who opposed Measure B) became one of the few straight porn producers to require condoms in her shoots, much to the consternation of some industry peers. "It just struck me we need to take a step back and look at how we can give people the safest work experience possible ... I can no longer roll the dice on my set," Taormino told CNN about her decision.[3] Porn professional Madison Young says, "As a director, I feel that creating a condom-optional policy for my talent works best. I shoot a lot of real-life couples that don't use condoms in their personal life so they choose not to use them. Also sometimes women who have latex allergies or experience discomfort from using condoms opt not to use them in their scene. But they always have that choice." As for arguments that condoms in porn might ruin the fantasy, Young replies, "I also feel that it's important to show on film that safer sex practices can be sexy."[4]

Because pornography production is legal in the state of California and because an estimated 80 percent of all legal porn is produced in Los Angeles County, the region provides an important yardstick for measuring prevention, testing, and response protocol. In contrast, although pornography is produced around the world, the health practices are harder to document, and very little has been written about global health conditions for porn performers. As of 2004, Brazil had become a destination for adult film production outside Los Angeles. The Brazilian porn industry considers testing to be expensive and unreliable, instead preferring condom use as prevention. But, in practice, many adult performers working in Brazil do not use condoms. According to the Associated Press, about 80 percent of Brazilian porn films are made with actors using condoms; however, Brazilian industry executives say that about 80 percent of *American companies* filming in Brazil require actors to film unprotected sex scenes.

### What Are the STI Testing Requirements for Porn Performers?

As of 2015, standard protocol for adult talent involves voluntary testing done every fourteen days. These tests are conducted at a variety of private testing sites, the bulk of which are in Los Angeles County, with an additional location in Las Vegas and another in Miami. Once tests are completed, the results are entered into the Performer Availability Screening Services (PASS), a database that is maintained by the Free Speech Coalition. Prior to a shoot, producers, directors, and the talent departments check the PASS database. The PASS data is also available to performers on request.

As of 2009, the gay male porn industry did not require testing. Given the gay male community's unique history with HIV, some were deeply concerned about stigma, discrimination, and the potential invasion of privacy that testing could involve. Rather than mandatory testing, gay porn producers proceeded on the assumption that many performers are HIV-positive. As early as 1989, gay porn became known for leading the way in condom-friendly, on-set policies, with Chi Chi

LaRue filming *Flexx*, the first porn movie using condoms in every scene. In 2004, Titan Media, one of the largest gay porn studios, announced it would not hire actors who have had unprotected sex in porn videos. By 2014, some gay studios such as Hot Desert Knight decided to offer bareback scenes and to also require testing protocol consistent with the straight industry standard.

The adult industry currently rejects legally enforced condom requirements, instead favoring a voluntary, multipronged strategy for STI prevention. In addition to current testing and reporting protocol (PASS), this strategy also includes biomedical prevention methods such as preexposure prophylaxis (PrEP)—a daily pill that prevents HIV infection from taking hold if a person is exposed to the virus. The industry's voluntary HIV/STI prevention strategy includes the choice to use condoms for those performers who prefer them, although this may not be practical unless industry standards shift toward widespread condom use. Many productions include on-set visual inspection of mouths, hands, and genitals for sores.

Medical evidence reports that using condoms alone in preventing HIV is between 70 percent and 87 percent effective. PrEP has been shown to reduce the risk of HIV transmission by a dramatically higher rate of over 92 percent, and the Centers for Disease Control (CDC) endorses its use in HIV prevention. In June 2015, the Los Angeles Board of Supervisors voted to begin providing Truvada (the market name for PrEP) to high-risk populations, specifically identifying Latino and black gay and bisexual men, and transgender people of color, as among those who would most benefit. Calling Truvada a "party drug" that would encourage more high-risk behavior, Michael Weinstein of the AHF and staunch opponent of the adult film industry was named by County officials as the one person responsible for most of the five-year delay in developing the PrEP program. (Weinstein denies he is the cause of this delay.)

The current (straight) industry standard includes testing every fourteen days for a panel of sexually transmitted conditions: chlamydia, gonorrhea, HIV, syphilis, hepatitis B, hepatitis C, and trichomoniasis. PASS testing facilities use blood tests to screen performers for syphilis and hepatitis B and C.

The Aptima HIV-1 test preferred by the adult industry tests plasma for the HIV virus and is FDA-approved to detect acute (meaning recent) infection. This is a far more accurate and effective test than enzyme-linked immunosorbent assay (ELISA) because Aptima can detect traces of the HIV virus within six to ten days of initial serotransmission. Everyday testing for HIV typically uses the Elisa/Western Blot, which has a three- to six-month incubation window. The "window period" refers to the time between infection and when a test can detect the presence of virus antibodies. Although the adult industry uses a far more sophisticated test for HIV, the fact remains that a person can become infected with the virus and still test negative for several days. Even with HIV and STI testing requirements in place, a person can be positive the very next day after a negative test, thus increasing the risk of transmission to others. The CDC caution that even with biweekly testing, it is possible for cases of HIV or other STIs to escape notice. Testing alone is not adequate prevention, the CDC explains, because infected performers could transmit these diseases for a period of time before an infection can be diagnosed.

Several additional problems with testing and response procedures have been raised. Among these problems is the fact that performers are required to pay for tests and vaccinations, which is inconsistent with Cal/OSHA standards that require employers to bear the cost of work-related health tests. There is discussion about shifting the cost of STI testing to the producers, rather than requiring the talent to pay, but this requirement is a bit tricky when workers are classified as independent contractors or freelancers rather than as employees.

Some argue that urine-only tests are insufficient, and even blood tests are not good enough. The point is made that swabs should be taken to test any mucus membranes that come in contact with body fluids. Current industry testing does not check for herpes, giardia, and the human papilloma virus (HPV), although many performers voluntarily test for HPV.

In addition, there are no global standards or consistent practices for testing or on-set safety. Early research on transnational health issues among porn actors published in the *International Journal of STD & AIDS* found that urine-only testing missed infections in 23 percent of cases in the United States. Similar results were apparent among adult performers in the United Kingdom. To be cleared to work, British porn actors must provide a negative urine test result from within the previous thirty days. Although no cases of HIV, syphilis, hepatitis B, or hepatitis C were found in this study, 38 percent were diagnosed with 77 STIs—and all performers said they'd had condomless sex while filming. Of the study's participants, 75 percent had at least one sexual partner outside of work; and only 10 percent used condoms consistently with their off-set partners. Furthermore, the researchers stressed that 60 percent of gonorrheal infections are detected only through oral and/ or rectal testing rather than by urine tests. Monthly screening and certification is required for adult performers to work in the United Kingdom, yet the study observed that STIs are common—or commonly undiscovered—in an industry where unprotected sex is the norm. These undiagnosed infections can be transmitted to sexual partners inside and outside the adult film industry.

### What Are Some Changes in STI Testing and Health Safety Protocol?

The adult industry testing standards change along with new science—and sometimes due to shifting political climates. For instance, Trep-Sure, a serological test for syphilis, was replaced by the Rapid Plasma Reagin (RPR) test for active performers; first-time performers were still required to have two Trep-Sure tests, fourteen days apart. Second, the Free Speech Coalition's PASS system switched from voluntary testing every thirty days to a biweekly standard. Third, according to Diane Duke of the FSC, plans were underway to begin using swabs to test for chlamydia and gonorrhea.

During a June 2010 California State OSHA Advisory Meeting about Bloodborne Pathogens in the Adult Film Industry, Robert Kim-Farley, Director of Communicable Disease Control and Prevention at LACDPH, reiterated that sexually transmitted infections are common among porn performers and often go undiagnosed. "The STD risks are increased by high-risk sexual practices on film sets including multiple partners over short time periods, ejaculation into the face, mucous membranes and mouth or eyes, internal vaginal and/or anal ejaculation, unprotected anal sex, double vaginal and double anal penetration, the sharing of sex toys, oral-anal contact, and oral sex after anal," stresses Kim-Farley. "STD risks are also increased by prolonged intercourse coupled with anogenital trauma, with bleeding and with menstruation and exposure to blood, semen, seminal and vaginal/cervical fluids."[5]

Kim-Farley's testimony is vivid and alarming, but researchers find it untrustworthy. Johns Hopkins epidemiologist Lawrence S. Mayer finds Kim-Farley's unreliable STI research so poorly documented and fundamentally flawed that he says it's hard to know where to even start in teasing out the problems. In Mayer's assessment, most of the evidence presented to Cal/OSHA by Robert Kim-Farley, as well as by Peter Kerndt, lacks transparency. Kim-Farley and Kerndt both fail to document their methodology—which is a standard practice in reputable research—and their analyses are without basis in epidemiology or science at large, Mayer challenges in his analysis made available by the Our Bodies Our Choice Campaign.

During a May 2015 Cal/OSHA hearing to update protocol in the adult film industry, the following mandate for minimizing workplace health risks was proposed: "The employer shall provide, at no cost to the employee, appropriate personal protective equipment such as, but not limited to, condoms, gloves for cleaning, and, if contact of the eyes with OPIM-STI is reasonably anticipated, eye protection." (OPIM refers to Other Potentially Infectious Materials.) This equipment must prevent blood or OPIM from contact with the performer's eyes, mouth, or other mucous membranes, or non-intact skin. In other words, the proposed revisions to the California State Standard could be interpreted to include not only condoms but goggles on porn sets: the former of which many continue to debate, and the latter of which many find simply ludicrous.

As *Xbiz Newswire* reported, the porn industry and public health officials oppose the Cal/OSHA proposal unless it is amended. Opponents include the Free Speech Coalition, the County of Los Angeles Commission on HIV, the American Civil Liberties Union, San Francisco AIDS Foundation, Equality California, the Gay Men's Health Crisis, and the Adult Performer Advocacy Committee.

Testifying before the Commission, Mario Perez, director of HIV and STD Programs for Los Angeles County, vocally opposed the proposed regulations. "As we think about the HIV and STD epidemics in our county, there continues to be . . . a disproportionate amount of energy and attention on an area that is not contributing to new HIV infections. . . . The epidemiology just isn't there for folks to continue to harp on this issue."[6]

Michael Weinstein, president of the AHF and a leading proponent of revising the state OSHA regulations, has called adult performers a threat to public health. Industry insiders respond that Weinstein's accusation is stigmatizing and counterproductive in terms of promoting medical safety. In 2015, Weinstein funded a ballot measure that, if passed, would pay him to review all porn produced in the state of California to make sure that condoms were used. Taxpayers would fund the salary for this "porn czar" position.

### What Happens If a Test Is Positive?

If an infection is reported after testing, the adult film industry implements a moratorium on filming to prevent further transmission. The industry has declared several production moratoriums in recent years for HIV concerns. In 2012, the industry stopped production due to positive syphilis test results. *The Guardian* reports that most moratoriums have been for infections that are "believed to have occurred in the private lives of actors rather than during film shoots."[7] But regardless of the initial source of exposure, a positive HIV or STI test in the adult industry means there is a risk of infecting others on the job.

If an industry performer tests positive for any of the conditions on the performer's test panel, the results are entered into the PASS database. An actor with positive test results would not be able to perform in an adult production. Sometimes, though, a performer has already appeared in a porn video and then subsequently tests positive. Under this circumstance, the Free Speech Coalition calls for a halt on porn productions until physicians determine that filming may continue.

The usual procedure for Free Speech Coalition PASS protocols involves a full two-week moratorium whenever there is a positive or reactive HIV test. A moratorium is called pending confirmation and testing of additional sexual partners and those with intimate contact. A "precautionary hold" is a shorter-term pause in filming pending the outcome of test results in concerning circumstances.

During a moratorium, a team of doctors re-tests the possible "patient zero" (meaning the initial person who tested positive) and then tests first-generation contacts and beyond, as necessary. Once this process is completed and the physicians determine it's safe to begin shooting again, the moratorium is lifted. During a filming shutdown, performers are obviously out of work—but the entire industry is impacted, from camera crews to makeup artists, video editors to production assistants. Many female performers use camming, stripping, or merchandise sales to offset this income loss. Far fewer revenue streams (especially stripping) are available to male talent.

### Are There Other Health Concerns Related to the Adult Film Industry?

In addition to concerns about transmission of HIV or other sexually transmitted infections, some worry about the prevalence and impact of breast implants, labiaplasty, increased anal sex rates, and the impact of waxing pubic hair in catering to fetish preferences or fashion trends. (I discussed the health risks related to Viagra and other male erection-enhancing drugs in chapter 4.) It is not uncommon for arguments about health issues to be blurred with personal opinion and moral or political qualms.

Among the fears about pornography's effects is the suggestion that porn performers are more likely to get cosmetic surgery such as breast implants. Select critics also worry that rigid beauty standards in mainstream pornography are linked to increased numbers of breast implants or labiaplasty among civilian women.

It is hard to ignore the changes in breast size or pubic hairstyles in comparing twentieth-century *Playboy* centerfolds or classic golden era porn films with today. Sheila Jeffreys writes in *Beauty and Misogyny: Harmful Cultural Practices in the West* that breast implant surgery is a harmful cultural practice and a form of mutilation. Jeffreys argues that pressure from pornography (and its male supremacist foundation) causes breast enlargement's popularity. Author Julia Long similarly reports in her book, *Anti-Porn,* that the increase of so-called beauty practices associated with the adult industry—removing pubic hair, breast augmentation, and labiaplasty—are the result of porn going mainstream.

## What Is Labiaplasty?

Labiaplasty refers to surgically trimming the labia minora and/or majora to make the skin folds smaller and more symmetrical. Sometimes the clitoral hood is also trimmed. According to the *Journal of Sexual Medicine*, 37 percent of women undergoing labiaplasty did so entirely for cosmetic (not functional) reasons. Medical risks from the procedure can include scarring, infection, bleeding, and nerve damage, although among those who've had the surgery, patient satisfaction ranges from 90 to 95 percent. Sexual satisfaction among women with labiaplasty is over 80 percent. Splashy headlines notwithstanding ("The Search for the Perfect Vagina"), it is hard to determine the rate of labiaplasty among porn performers or to prove that pornography causes labiaplasty among the general population.

It is also difficult to prove that heterosexual male preference is behind any trend toward the missing labia minora in pornographic images of women's vulvas. There is strong evidence suggesting that soft porn magazines such as *Playboy*, *Penthouse*, or Australia's *Picture* intentionally select female models with small inner labia or airbrush them out before publication.

But, in a strange twist of politics meets aesthetics, obscenity law may be a large factor in these labial matters. The Australian Classification Board allows "discreet genital detail" but no "genital emphasis" for soft porn to be classified as "unrestricted" and therefore available for sale to those under the age of eighteen. By airbrushing labia, magazines can avoid overt genital emphasis (i.e., showing pink) to meet the standards for legal publication. At the same time, this aesthetic or editorial decision incurs social critique. In any case, the fact is that there are a wide variety of genital size and shapes on display in pornography.

Still, a 2011 exposé in *The Guardian* squarely blames the rise of Internet pornography for increasing numbers of women seeking "designer labia." Reporting in a panicky tone that medical experts "have sounded the alarm over soaring rates of labiaplasty," *The Guardian* cites research from King's College London suggesting that increased exposure to online pornography "may be driving up surgery rates to unprecedented levels."[8] In the United Kingdom, the number of labiaplasty performed by the National Health Service (NHS) tripled from 1998 to 2008. The *British Journal of Obstetrics and Gynaecology* revealed that between 2008 and 2009, there was a nearly 70 percent increase in the number of women undergoing labiaplasty. (This rate accounts only for surgeries covered by the NHS and did not include private sector procedures, which are not audited or regulated.)

However, an increase in labiaplasty (or breast augmentation) and easier access to pornography does not prove that the latter causes the former. After collecting data from more than a thousand participants from twenty-five countries, Bethany Jones and Camille Nurka found that most women are happy with their vulvas. Their 2015 article published in the journal *Porn Studies* explains that although viewing pornography was linked with open-mindedness toward labiaplasty, watching porn did not predict labial satisfaction. This finding casts "doubt on a linear framework that positions pornography as the main driver for female genital cosmetic surgery."[9] Industry insiders also caution that the brouhaha regarding labiaplasty may be overblown.

The US data for "vaginal rejuvenation" suggests this procedure accounts for only about 0.2 percent of all cosmetic surgeries in the country. The argument against plastic surgery also presupposes that cosmetic alteration is unnatural, and is therefore wrong. Adult industry professional Danny Wylde suggests that another way of looking at the issue is that "people with all types of careers choose to augment their bodies ... such as a football player training all day until he's sore.... If your job is based on looking a certain way, it's no surprise that you would put in effort to keep up that look as a means of career maintenance and advancement."[10]

### Is There a Problem with Anal Sex?

"Career maintenance," however, does not answer the questions involved with the anal sex debate. *Pornland* author Gail Dines asserts that gonzo porn is causing more men to demand anal sex from women. There is also concern about this peer pressure among teens.

Researchers at the London School of Hygiene and Tropical Medicine who interviewed 130 teenagers in England, between the ages of 16 and 18 and from diverse social backgrounds, found that anal sex is commonly depicted in straight pornography and is increasingly practiced among young people. The motivation for engaging in anal sex appeared to be competition among boys and to emulate what they see in porn. The girls shared that they'd experienced instances of non-consensual penetration in a "try-and-see-approach" that boys often used, anticipating that the girl would not stop them. "The qualitative study found that anal heterosex appeared to be 'painful, risky and coercive, particularly for women,' while males spoke of being expected to persuade or coerce reluctant partners."

Unprotected anal sex is a high-risk activity in regard to STIs. The concise term for sexual coercion is rape. The British researchers therefore emphasize the urgent need for public discussions about harm reduction, mutuality, and consent to diminish risky health practices and normalized coercion regarding anal heterosex. But, they caution, "the 'pornography' explanation seems partial at best."[11] (In fact the authors found other important, non-porn-related reasons that explained young people's motivations to have anal sex. In a US-based study, teens who take "virginity pledges" were found to be more likely to engage in unprotected anal sex compared to their non-pledging peers.)

### Is Waxing Dangerous?

Given an upsurge in pornography that often features "pube-less" genitals, the safety of waxing or shaving pubic hair has also emerged as a public health debate. Indiana University researchers Debby Herbenick and Vanessa Schick, coauthors of *Read My Lips*, found in 2011 that nearly 60 percent of American women between 18 and 24—and almost 50 percent of women between 25 and 29—wax, shave, or trim their pubic hair. Of course, these practices are subject to change, with fashion magazines announcing "Pubic Hair Is Back!"

Shaving, trimming, or waxing pubic hair (in porn or in everyday life) can be understood as an aesthetic decision—and one that is subject to change. Cultural critics argue, though, that social demands for grown women to look like prepubescent girls is infantilizing and disempowering for adults. This demand for adult women to shave or wax also eroticizes female children, which thus contributes to child sexual abuse.

As for the men? Comparisons of men and women's preferences about pubic hair found that genital grooming is common among young adults in the United States. However, there is a distinction. Men are far more likely than women to want hair-free sexual partners (60 percent of men compared to 24 percent of women). When it comes to removing pubic hair, 50 percent of women report they are hair-free, but only 19 percent of men report the same. Concurrently, more women reported unpleasant side effects from hair-removal practices.

The documented risks for waxing include infections; increased risk of herpes or HPV as a result of skin trauma; burns from hot wax (or reactions to product applied in delicate regions); and an increased risk of sexually transmitted molluscum contagiosum, a viral skin condition also known as water warts. Similar side effects can occur from anal bleaching, which is also a featured practice among porn performers and has trickled into the mainstream. The pornography industry is often blamed for Brazilian waxes (and anal bleaching) gaining in popularity, but it is hard to prove the link.

### What Are the Debates about Pornography Addiction?

"Addiction" is a powerful term often used casually in everyday vernacular to describe a host of conditions from watching a favorite TV show to intractable overeating to heroin dependence. But although the addiction model is frequently used to describe dysfunctional porn use, it is not clear from the science that addiction is the correct term to use. Addiction means very specific things to brain and behavior researchers; and there is robust debate over whether excessive, impulsive, or compulsive pornography use is actually an addiction.

Patrick Carnes is one of the leading experts on sex addiction and considered a pioneer in the field. According to Carnes, pornography addiction is one form of broader sex addiction. The signs of addiction include using sexual obsession and fantasy as a primary coping strategy, out-of-control sexual behavior, experiencing severe consequences due to pornography use—such as job or relationship problems—and an inability to stop despite these adverse consequences. Elements of porn addiction also consist of an ongoing desire or effort to limit porn use behavior and severe mood changes when these efforts are ineffective. Other behavioral clues are secretive habits such as hiding Internet porn histories, withdrawing from social contact with others, and losing sleep due to porn use. In sum, pornography addiction causes distress to the porn addict. The addiction creates distancing from others while intimacy deteriorates.

Porn addiction involves compulsively reading pornography, obsessively watching it, or chronically thinking about pornography—all with detrimental effect on a person's life. Experts state that the guidelines for drug addiction mirror the experience people report with pornography addiction: namely, failure in resisting the impulse to use porn (or drugs), increased tension just before using porn (or drugs), and pleasure or relief at the time of using porn (or drugs). Repeated attempts to reduce or stop using pornography are met with failure, and the addict builds a tolerance that requires increasingly intense content or frequency to get the desired effect.

According to Patrick Carnes, the root of pornography addiction begins in childhood when there is abuse or neglect. In this case, healthy exploration with porn goes beyond curiosity or self-soothing masturbation. When addiction develops, sex—or pornography—is confused for the nurturing that is missing from a child's life. As Carnes writes in his book, *In the Shadows of the Net: Breaking Free of Compulsive Online Sexual Behavior,* this confusion about porn eventually becomes an addiction and can lead to other, more harmful, sexual behaviors. Compulsively masturbating to pornography can turn into anonymous sex, risky hookups, and even illegal activities, says Carnes.

Australian researcher Michael Flood is more cautious about these links. Flood warns that the addiction model is dangerous if we lean on the analogy between pornography use and drug use and assume that one taste means you're hooked. For some people, pornography is clearly habitual and compulsive, with negative effects on other areas of their life, Flood explains. At the same time, however, we ought to be wary of medicalizing or pathologizing porn use, says Flood. We ought to be careful about assuming, for example, that any teen pornography use (or powerful interest in sex) is automatically a problem. "In addition," Flood writes, "notions of pornography use as 'addictive' or 'compulsive' may divert attention from questions regarding [porn] users' agency and responsibility."[12]

The *Diagnostic and Statistical Manual of Mental Disorders* (*DSM*), the official psychiatric guide that defines and diagnoses mental-health conditions, is now in its fifth edition. Known as the *DSM–V,* the book does not include a definitive entry on hypersexuality, which is the clinical term for sex addiction. In contrast with Dr. Carnes's theories about addiction, the *DSM–V* instead lists hypersexuality as among several conditions that need more research. If hypersexuality is not formally recognized as a psychiatric condition, then it stands to reason that neither sex addiction nor is its close cousin, porn addiction, are bona fide diagnostic terms.

In an effort to untangle the puzzle around dysfunctional porn use, one study conducted by the University of Cambridge investigated the neural correlations between sexual cues and compulsive sexual behavior. In short, the findings were that among people exhibiting compulsive sexual behavior, pornography triggers brain activity in ways that are similar to the effect of drugs on addicts' brains. But even these researchers avoid claiming that pornography is inherently addictive. The study also found a correlation between brain activity and age, for instance, with younger patients showing the highest levels of neural response to pornography.

Among the experts who strongly disagree with the porn addiction model are Timothy Fong, MD, and Nicole Prause, PhD, researchers at the UCLA's Semel Institute for Neuroscience and Human Behavior. As Prause explains, the scholarship on porn addiction is complicated by misunderstandings about addiction, often combined with religious anxiety and financial motivation.

The way addiction is defined in scientific research is different from the public's understanding of addictions, explains Prause. What's more, a very large money-driven treatment industry has grown around so-called porn addiction. *The Daily Beast* reports the stakes around this issue are so high that neuroscience researchers such as Fong, Prause, and Vaughn Steele have received calls to retract their published articles, legal threats, and emails telling them to kill themselves.

Despite such threats, the UCLA-based research team published their findings in *Biological Psychology*. This article reports that people with trouble controlling their porn use did not show a typical neural response to sexual images. Addicts typically have *increased* brain activity when they are exposed to the source of their addiction. But the male and female "porn addicts" in this study had *decreased* brain activity when they were shown visual sexual stimuli. These findings do not mean people are faking a problem if they say they're having trouble with compulsive porn use. It means that addiction is the wrong treatment model for the problem. And, if compulsive porn use is not an addiction, yet is being handled as such, treatment providers could be harming patients not helping them. A constructive alternative to the addiction model is to focus on sexual compulsivity, Prause suggests.

### Are There Links between Pornography Use and Erectile Dysfunction?

Short of addiction or compulsive use problems, there is the belief that pornography is linked to erectile dysfunction among heterosexual men who frequently view sexual stimuli. The argument is that men who watch a lot of porn are influenced by unrealistic portrayals of female sexuality and of women's bodies. This effect is thought to be so strong that compulsive porn users become unable to get aroused by their female partners.

An article in *Sexual Medicine* puts this concern to rest (although it does not investigate women's sexual response rates). This research revealed that regularly using pornography actually enhanced (male) participants' desire for their (female) sexual partners. The findings conclude that more hours viewing pornography was unrelated to men's ability to get or maintain an erection with a partner and that watching porn was related to a stronger desire for sex with a partner.

# 9

# CHILDREN AND TEENS USING PORNOGRAPHY

The issue of children and teens accessing pornography is often fraught with distress and debate. There are those who worry that easy access to porn causes harm among today's youth. Will children who see porn grow up to be sexist? Will they make dangerous sexual decisions? Will relationships and self-image suffer? Is sexting a form of pornography? Perhaps online porn heralds the end of morality.

Research and conventional wisdom indicate good reason for concern when it comes to children and teens viewing porn. At the same time, there is research suggesting that collective moral panic undermines rational and effective responses to these matters. Some data may even blow the issue out of proportion. Every generation has had its share of explicit content and sexually curious kids, pundits point out. And yet society continues to thrive.

Muddling the conversation is that research about college-age young people—or emerging adults—is often blended along with discussions about those who are legally still children. In fairness to matters of health and well-being, it makes sense to clarify distinctions between those under 18 and those who are legally adults. In this chapter, therefore, I focus specifically on pornography use among children and teens. Regardless of legal maturity, however, there is a strong case to be made for the constructive aspects of age-appropriate education and open dialogue in promoting healthy, consensual sexuality.

### How Many Youth Are Watching Porn? And How Old Are They When They Start?

As recently as the 1980s, sneaking a look at pornography generally meant kids finding a glossy magazine that was tucked away by an older adult. With online access to every imaginable form of sexual content, some adults fear all that has changed. The ease of access to explicit content is far different now than in the past. It is easy to accidentally stumble across lewd images intended for an adult audience. One click on a box asking if the viewer is an adult is all it takes to access free porn sites. And even the sites with paywalls have enough free teasers to comprise a fair amount of exposure to sexually explicit material. The question is, how young are children first seeing online pornography? How much porn are they watching? What type of content are they finding? And what effect does pornography have on children's psychosexual and interpersonal development?

A number of researchers have investigated the average age at which teenagers first see pornography, the prevalence of teens viewing porn, and the impact this has on adolescent development. The results of some studies are routinely repeated—but dubious.

One frequently repeated figure claims that the average age a boy first sees pornography today is 11 years old. CNN, NBC, and other news outlets around the country have relied on this number. When Senator Blanche Lincoln (D-Ark.) introduced the Internet Safety and Child Protection Act to Congress, she cited this often-used statistic. Yet a 2008 study led by Chiara Sabina found that the average age of first exposure to pornography was actually age 14.3 for boys and 14.8 for girls (with a noticeable uptick in first exposure among 11-year-old boys).

Developmentally speaking, there is a significant distinction between an 11-year-old preteen and a teenager who is 14-going-on-15 years old. It seems that the dubious claim got its start from a 2005 article in *The Boston Globe* titled "The Secret Life of Boys."

*The Boston Globe*'s source for this figure traces back to an organization called Family Safe Media, a small firm in Provo, Utah, that "is in the business of scaring parents into buying software to protect their kids from Internet smut," writes Seth Lubove in *Forbes*. And here is where the sources get even murkier.

Jared Martin is the owner of Family Safe Media. Martin says he got his porn statistics from Internet Filter Review, a website that recommends content-blocking software. Internet Filter Review is run by Utah-based entrepreneur Jerry Ropelato, who writes anti-porn polemics such as "Tricks Pornographers Play" and has published a variety of unsupported statistics. One of Ropelato's signature claims is that children between ages of 12 and 17 are the largest demographic group of people viewing online porn. However, this simply isn't true.

Ropelato insists his data is reliable and says he got the age-11 figure from *The Drug of the New Millennium*. This is a self-published book about the dangers of pornography written by a self-described former porn addict, Mark Kastleman, who is also from Utah. " 'I don't remember where I got that from,' Kastleman says breezily. 'That is a very common statistic.' " And this is where the trail goes cold, *Forbes* magazine reports.[1]

Despite this widely repeated claim that young boys' first exposure to porn is at age 11, Michele Ybarra of Internet Solutions for Kids in Irvine, California, and Kimberly Mitchell of the Crimes Against Children Research Center at the University of New Hampshire find that "the vast major-ity (87 percent) of youth who report looking for sexual images online are 14 years of age or older, when it is developmentally appropriate to be sexually curious."[2]

A survey commissioned by the United Kingdom's BBC revealed in 2014 that 25 percent of young people watched Internet porn by the age of 12. Only 7 percent had seen porn by the time they were 10 or younger. One-third of the youth said they came across pornography by accident. The rest claimed they intentionally used porn to answer questions they had about sex. Whereas one out of five of the young women questioned said they had never seen Internet pornography, only 4 percent of young men gave the same answer, leading the BBC's Jameela Jamil to comment that she worries about "the new generation of men whose first real introduction to sex is what they see on their laptop."[3] In a study of Canadian teenagers, there was a similar disparity, with 90 percent of the boys and 70 percent of the girls claiming they'd seen pornography at least once. Boys aged 13 and 14 living in rural areas were the most likely of their age group to access porn.

It is hard to know whether self-reported gender differences are accurate reflections of who's using porn. It could be this disparity results from girls' fears of admitting to seeing pornography given cultures of slut-shaming that stigmatize female sexual desire. Be that as it may, more than half of those surveyed by the BBC said that seeing pornography at such a young age impacted their sexual expectations. Many claimed that young men expected young women to act like what they see in pornography.

A 2015 study of teenagers from age 14 to 17 found that boys were generally positive about the images they saw in pornography. But in contrast, this research on "Adolescents' Experience With Sex on the Web" found that most of the girls thought sexually explicit websites were dumb, gross, or demeaning to women. US research consistently finds that a minority of young female partners of males who regularly use pornography feel like it is a form of infidelity. Still, this gender analysis refers to young women *in relation to* young men, and it is difficult to discern the impact of social norms on boys' bravado and girls' more dainty replies. What remains noticeably missing from this research is sufficient attention to queer sex, autonomous female sexuality, and girls response to—or use of—pornography.

### What Are Key Concerns about the Effects on Teens Watching Porn?

There is a very real difference between healthy sexual curiosity and unwanted—or even forced—exposure to pornography. *Pediatrics*, the professional journal of the American Academy of Pediatrics, reports that 42 percent of Internet users between the ages of 10 and 17 said they had seen online porn in the previous twelve months. Of those youth, 66 percent said the exposure to online porn was unwanted. HealthyChildren.org reminds that child sexual abuse is any sexual activity that a child cannot comprehend or consent to. This includes exposing children to pornography.

In addition to the problem of abusive and unwanted exposure, parents, educators, and community members worry that pornography hypersexualizes young girls, creates expectations of masculine sexual conquest, and leads to risky sexual behavior. There is fear that pornography promotes female sexual accommodation, objectification, and *self*-objectification. There is concern over the fact that children or teens may use pornography as sex education, thus leading to misguided expectations about bodies, sexuality, and sexual pleasure. There is even distress about the possibility of teenage porn addiction. A study on Dutch youth concluded that although more research was needed, it appeared there was a significant link between watching pornography and engaging in "adventurous" and "transactional" sex.

Anecdotal evidence abounds in arguments about pornography's impact on the sexual landscape, such as claims that "the Internet has made boys porn-ready for dating," with one young man going so far as to strangle a young woman on their first date because he thought "this was normal and acceptable behavior based on the pornography he had viewed."[4] Psychologist William Pollack expresses a concern shared by many. As the author of the popular book *Real Boys*, Pollack says, "boys are looking for a normal aspect of what girls look like, biologically, but they're getting this hard-core movie-industry type of material. If they didn't have an interest in it before, they are drawn into a world that goes beyond the normal curiosity."[5]

Like any media genre, it is unfathomable that pornography would have no impact on its young viewers. Yet beyond conjecture about the effect porn has on teens, what does the data indicate about how teenagers handle this information?

The CDC reports that compared with the early 1990s, before online porn was widely available, more recent rates of teen intercourse and sexual assault have declined considerably, and teen condom use has increased. Between 1991 and 2009, the teen birth rate dropped by 33 percent. This link is not proof that Internet porn causes an increase in safer sex or a decrease in rape. It does indicate, however, that moral panic surrounding teen access to online pornography may be misdirected.

Swedish professors Sven-Axel Månsson and Lotta Löfgren-Mårtenson say that in their study of adolescents, most teens are able to separate sexual fantasy in pornography from real-life sex. Månsson and Löfgren-Mårtenson write in their article "Lust, Love and Life" that of 73 working-class Swedish teens ages 14 to 20, "most participants had acquired the skills to navigate the pornographic landscape in a sensible manner. Most had the ability to distinguish between pornographic fantasies on the one hand, and real sexual interactions and relationships on the other." Månsson points out that this response presupposes that all the teens had sexual experiences—and not all of them had.

The girls in this study revealed more ambivalence toward pornography than the boys, with the majority of girls claiming that porn was repulsive. Of the one-third of the girls who found it interesting and exciting, none announced that opinion widely, especially to the boys. Their fear was of ending up with a "bad reputation" and being slut-shamed simply for liking pornography or for being curious about it.

In 2014, *The Journal of Sex Research* published an article titled "Without Porn I Wouldn't Know Half the Things I Know Now." Based on this qualitative research investigating porn use among black and Hispanic teens, the following themes emerged.

First, the youth surveyed said they mainly watched pornography that featured one-on-one sexual intercourse rather than group sex. However, they also reported having seen extreme pornography (e.g., public humiliation or incest). Second, these 16- to 18-year-olds reported watching pornography on home computers or smartphones. That is fairly predictable; but perhaps more surprising, they also said that pornography was frequently watched in school. Of 9- to 16-year-olds participating in a British study, 91 percent said they watched porn at school.

The youth reported watching porn for entertainment, sexual stimulation, instructional purposes, and because they were bored. Many copied what they saw in pornography during their own sexual encounters. Pressure to imitate pornography, or to make their own porn, were elements present in some unhealthy dating relationships.

A great deal of public emphasis on teens using porn has focused exclusively on boys. Simon Lajeunesse, from the University of Montreal, had to rethink his research design when he was unable to find any young men under the age of 20 who hadn't seen porn. Without this control group, there was no way to draw comparisons about pornography's effects. So, instead of observing the impact of pornography on men's sexuality and perceptions of gender, Lajeunesse shifted his focus to study men's porn-viewing habits. He discovered that, on average, single men watch pornography three times a week for 40 minutes. Men in committed relationships watch far less porn. These men watch an average 1.7 times a week for 20 minutes. Lajeunesse also found that most boys seek out porn by the time they're 10, an age at which they are most sexually curious. Again, though, this contradicts other findings that the average age of first exposure to porn is around 14 years old.

During a Ted Talk by Philip Zimbardo on the so-called "demise of guys," the psychologist famous for the Stanford Prison Experiment explained that high-speed access to pornography means that "boys' brains are being digitally rewired in a totally new way for change, novelty, excitement and constant arousal. That means they're totally out of sync in traditional classes [in school], which are analog, static, interactively passive. They're also totally out of sync in romantic relationships, which build gradually and subtly."

Building on Zimbardo's points, Gary Wilson presented a TedX talk in Glasgow, Scotland, titled "The Great Porn Experiment," alerting the audience about what supposedly happens when children grow up with unlimited access to porn. Wilson, a physiology teacher with an interest (if not training) in neuroscience, explains that adolescents are extremely impressionable. And adolescent brain plasticity combined with online pornography creates sexually dysfunctional young men. Because of the impact of high-speed Internet porn access, by the time teenage boys turn 22, their sexual tastes have become deep grooves in their brain, Wilson proclaims. The constant dopamine release from chronically watching porn leads to erectile dysfunction, even among relatively young men. Furthermore, Wilson conjectures, these "brain grooves" can create alarming conditions for young men if porn use has escalated to watching ever-more extreme images or if the porn young men are watching does not match their sexual orientation.

It is worth noting that arguments such as Wilson's, although possibly enticing at the outset, are built on flimsy science that reveals more about sexist and heterosexist assumptions than proven neuroscience about addiction and pornography. It also feeds into moral panic about teen porn use that may be unfounded. Although Lajeunesse discovered that most boys seek out porn by age 10, they grew into reasonable young men who "said they supported gender equality and felt victimized by rhetoric demonizing pornography." (In his TedX talk, Gary Wilson quotes Lajeunesse's first point but conveniently ignores the latter emphasis.)

Children and teens might come across extreme sexual images, but Lajeunesse found that boys quickly discard what they don't like or find offensive. As young men, they continue to look for porn content that is in tune with their image of sexuality. "Pornography hasn't changed [young men's] perception of women or their relationship which they all want as harmonious and fulfilling as possible," says Lajeunesse. "Those who could not live out their fantasy in real life with their partner simply set aside the fantasy. The fantasy is broken in the real world and men don't want their partner to look like a porn star."[6]

Lajeunesse refutes the perverse effect often attributed to pornography. Adult men who sexually assault do not need pornography to be violent criminals. "If pornography had the impact that many claim it has," says Lajeunesse, "you would just have to show heterosexual films to a homosexual to change his sexual orientation."[7] And clearly, this is not the case.

Australian researcher Michael Flood hesitates in letting porn off the hook. Flood writes that being exposed to pornography helps to sustain young people's belief in unhealthy, sexist ideas about sex and relationships. This does not prove that pornography *causes* sexism; but clearly mainstream pornography continuously presents unhealthy cultural messages. According to Flood, the context of exposure to porn, and the nature of youth engagement with it—intentional, accidental, curious, or compulsive—impacts what sort of effects pornography has on children and teens.

It is not as if children and teenagers are blank slates at the time they see pornography. It is likely, Flood writes, that the effect of seeing pornography is mediated by other factors, such as education or family life, all of which impacts how young viewers interpret and evaluate the material.[8] As Robert Weiss points out, porn use is probably not a concern for most. The majority who view pornography will do so without serious later-life problems, just as most teens who try alcohol and recreational drugs don't become alcoholics or addicts. But on the other hand, states Weiss (who founded the Sexual Recovery Institute), vulnerable teens who may have emotional and psychological challenges are absolutely at risk if they experiment with pornography.[9] Dr. Irene Peters echoes this point. Peters, who trains sexuality educators, remarks that part of adolescence involves experimenting with taboo adult behavior. For most youth, viewing pornography is not harmful. Those teenagers who are "most likely to be affected by pornography are ones with poor parental supervision in abusive households." There is a great deal of "hysteria and scapegoating around pornography,"[10] Peters says. Pornography gets blamed for a great number of social ills.

In spite of fears about the ease with which children can access fetish or unfamiliar forms of human sexuality online, it is not clear that accessing these images is linked to negative behavior among teens. Researchers at Middlesex University London could not establish a causal relationship between pornography use among underage viewers and risky sexual behavior such as unprotected sex, use of alcohol or drugs in sex, and having sex at younger ages.[11] In answering how the ubiquity of online porn affects the sexual development of children and teens, the scientific consensus is that "we have no idea," writes Amanda Hess for *Slate*.

### Is Sexting a Form of Pornography?

Sexting refers to sending, receiving, or forwarding sexually explicit messages, photographs, or images using a cell phone, computer, or other digital device.

According to a 2008 survey, one in five US teenagers had sent a sexually explicit photo of themselves to someone else or posted one online. By 2012, a study in southeast Texas found that 30 percent of teens were texting nude photos or sending them by email. Of the 700 British youth surveyed in 2015, 12 percent said they had participated in making a sexually explicit video. Another study in Texas again found that about 30 percent of teens surveyed had sent naked pictures of themselves using social media, and 60 percent of teens had been asked for one.

It's incredibly easy for sexted images to go viral and become widely distributed by phone or the Internet. The consequence that can result from subsequent cyberbullying and online harassment is profound, even causing its victims to experience depression, anxiety, and severe isolation. There have been several cases of teen suicide, such as 15-year-old Audrie Pott and 17-year-old Rehtaeh Parsons, who were victims of relentless taunts and bullying after photos from their brutal sexual assaults were circulated.

The problem is not consensual sexting but the nonconsensual exploitation and exposure of these digital media. The criminal justice system has been slow to respond to the problem. In the process of figuring out what to do, courts in the United States, Australia, and elsewhere around the globe have been known to use child pornography laws to criminalize teens involved with consensually or non-consensually sexting photos or video content.

### What Are Parental Controls—and Are They Effective?

Out of concern for children and teens accessing inappropriate or harmful sexual media, parents have turned to a growing industry in finding ways to control access to the Internet. Parental controls include features to restrict access times, block specific websites, or filter Internet access using URL keywords. Parents can also view Internet usage history, but because this is one of the easiest measures for kids to bypass, there is other software available that provides ways to record every keystroke made on the computer. Some parental control measures maintain logs of which websites are visited, which files are accessed, and even record instant messages. There is software that can be configured to automatically record screen captures of each Internet session.

But if an innocuous keyword search can accidentally pull up a fetish porn site, it is also true that parental control measures can block access to search terms used for legitimate school research or other information-finding ventures.

As an alternative solution to underage access to sexually explicit material, Steven C. Brown suggests we pay more attention to locking down porn piracy. The financial effects of piracy on the adult entertainment industry are well documented. But there is another angle to explore. Online piracy brings sexual content to people who are far too young to understand it, Brown points out in his 2014 *Porn Studies* article.

The London School of Economics confirms that engaged parents who teach their children online safety tools can make a big impact on behavior. Filtering software *alone* has no significant impact on 9- to 14-year-olds and is even associated with increased harm for 15- and 16-year-olds. Journalist Peggy Drexler comments that from adolescence on, blocking and filtering pornography are simply forms of parental denial. When curiosity and "biological urgency meets technological capability, the only weapon is to construct a frame of reference; a way to process things past generations have never seen. How families approach that is an individual decision. But there is a fundamental and consistent message: porn is not sex. It's a commercial depiction of sex that has nothing to do with real (non-digital) human relationships."[12] To paraphrase what many adult performers have said about their industry, learning about sex from pornography makes as much sense as learning how to drive by watching NASCAR races.

## What Is Porn Literacy—and How Can It Help?

Porn literacy is a form of education focused on more accurately understanding media messaging about gender, race, sexual consent, and body image. In terms of pornography, the goal of media literacy is to promote valuable discussions about "personal integrity, gender equality, human rights, and safer sex."[13] Age-appropriate media literacy promotes healthy sexual development and preventive solutions to sexual harm. Media literacy provides crucial skills that enable children and teens to identify sexism, misogyny, and racism in all forms of pop culture, including pornography.

As a generation of porn watchers comes of age, it is arguably to society's benefit that youth are taught a kind of "porn literacy" that encourages a better understanding of what constitutes mutually consensual sex in real life. The evidence points to this need. Of Australian youth, 64 percent say they learned about sex from pornography. Youth Health Program Officer Christina Self suggests that one of the reasons that teens are relying on porn may be due to the fact that sexuality education in the schools is avoiding what many young people really want to know about—how to look, how to act, and how to give or experience pleasure during sex.

Deriving information about sex from online porn means that teenagers can come away with skewed perspectives and wild misunderstandings about what it means to have sex. One 15-year-old boy said, "I just don't understand why my girlfriend doesn't like it when I call her bitch during sex." Australian Sexual Health Services' Schools Coordinator Sue Dimitrijevich shared that they receive questions such as the one from 13-year-old girls asking can they can have sex if they haven't had a Brazilian.[14]

Many people fear that when children or teens see pornography, it will trigger increased and riskier sexual activity, aggressive behavior, or trauma. There is concern that pornography portrays human bodies and gender relations in unhealthy ways. Censoring youth access to pornography through filtering programs and other parental controls has been shown to be ineffective. For every filtering program, there is a workaround, sometimes as easy as going to a friend's house. Second, the American Academy of Pediatrics makes clear that abstinence-only education is a waste of time especially "when the media have become such an important source of information" about sexual activity. Because pornography is one aspect of media, it holds that promoting porn abstinence is also an unwise strategy.[15]

As the *Journal of Sex Research* describes it, parents are generally unsupportive of youth's use of pornography but underequipped to talk about it with their kids. Irene Peters, author of *Pornography: Discussing Sexually Explicit Images*, stresses that it is important for parents and other responsible adults to talk with teens about pornography. Accurate and honest information gives adolescents the tools for increasing what Peters calls "sexual resilience."

Various scholars and government agencies have considered this concept of porn literacy and sexual resilience—meaning teaching the skills to understand sexuality, desire, beauty, and consent. Michael Flood writes that "protecting children from sexual harm does not mean protecting children from sexuality. In fact, maintaining children's sexual ignorance fosters sexual abuse and poor sexual and emotional health. However, pornography is a poor sex educator."[16] To his point, after finding that a significant number of children have access to sexually explicit images, a 2013 report by the UK's Office of the Children's Commissioner called for urgent action to develop educational curriculum that helps build young people's resilience to pornography. The report also called on Britain's Department for Education to ensure that all schools provide effective information about sex and relationships—including education about sexting, pornography, and how to use the Internet safely.

A Danish professor agrees with the sentiment of the UK report, stating that talking with teenagers about pornography would make them more critical consumers. Sex education has been mandatory in Denmark since 1970, and pornography is already included in the curriculum in several Danish schools. But Christian Graugaard of Aalborg University proposes taking this one step further. His proposal is to have trained teachers critically discuss pornography as part of a sensible sex education program. These discussions would begin with eighth and ninth graders, ages 15 and 16, respectively, Graugaard told *The Guardian*. (Fifteen is the legal age of sexual consent in Denmark.) This educational programming would involve conversations about pornography and would include showing examples in class as well. According to one Nordic study, 99 percent of boys and 86 percent of girls in Scandinavia have already seen pornographic films by the time they're 16 years old. "We know from research that a vast majority of teenagers have seen porn at an early age—so it's not a question of introducing youngsters to porn," Graugaard added. Porn may actually offer a variety of educational properties; it can even be feminist; and, depending on the production emphasis, pornography can promote diversity, says Graugaard. Yet mainstream pornography can easily exclude or stereotype various body types, races, genders, and sexualities. "Open-minded, constructive dialogue is the best way to make sure that teens are able to make meaningful decisions for themselves," says Graugaard. "It's not our job to scare off teenagers, rather we should encourage them to explore the joys of sexuality in a safe way and on their own terms—instead of turning our backs on them."[17]

Associate Pastor Cameron Beyenberg, who works with youth at a Southern California church, affirms this perspective. In working with young people between the ages of 14 and 18, Beyenberg notes that teens have a lot of questions about pornography, and they really want to talk about the issues— even if some of the teens are initially shy about it. It doesn't help that pornography has been such a taboo topic in the church, he adds. Personally, Pastor Beyenberg hopes the frank conversations will lead to abstinence from pornography. But the fact is, he notes, the average teen is already watching it; and this raises important issues about sexual consent, body image, and gender roles. Without a chance to talk openly about pornography, it leaves maturing teens with flooding hormones and easily available pornography. This combo can create a conflict between body image, gender-role expectations, and teens' sense of self. Beyenberg hopes education and conversation will help in better understanding these issues.

David Segal, writing for the *New York Times*, emphasized the fact that causal evidence between pornography and subsequent sexual choices is inconclusive; meaning, for example, that watching anal sex does not necessarily cause teens to engage in it. Quantifying "exposure" and "harm" is difficult for researchers, plus there are serious ethical problems with conducting research about the effects that pornography has on teens.[18] However, when teens have questions about pornography and they lack access to education, experts point out that the risk for teen confusion and misinformation about sexual health, self-image, and consent deserves consideration. Furthermore, there is emerging evidence that quantifies porn's effects on teens.

One research team led by Renata Arrington-Sanders found that pornography may play a key role in the lives of sexually active black gay youth. When there is limited school or family-based sex education to serve as a resource for sexual behavior, pornography becomes a prime source of information for learning about sexual activity. The 15- to 19-year-old teens in this study described using porn to understand sexual performance and sensation. The young gay teens said porn specifically helped them understand activities such as topping, bottoming, or barebacking.

Another study of sexual activity among heterosexual youth found a significant amount of condomless, coerced, or painful anal intercourse.[19] Given that many of the youth in this survey refer to pornography as the catalyst for engaging in unprotected or coerced anal intercourse, and given that 60 percent of British students surveyed claim they get their sex education from pornography,[20] it would make sense to include frank conversations about porn literacy in comprehensive sex education for teens.

# 10

# THE FUTURE OF PORN

The pornography industry is known to be an early adopter of technology that helps drive change across broader society. Pornography is also known for ensconcing racist, patriarchal stereotypes in a sexy package. It can promote pleasure, or even progressive change, in terms of body acceptance and sexual expression. Technology, politics, and commerce continue shifting the landscape of the pornography industry. The question is, *how so?* What is going to happen to pornography in the future?

Although there is no crystal ball to predict the future trends in porn, there are indicators that combine to tell an interesting story. To start, *Playboy* is getting out of the porn business while crowdfunding is getting *into* it. In an effort to cut costs, reduce staff, and increase profits, *Playboy* announced in 2009 that, except for editorial duties, it would outsource all of its operations to American Media, Inc. In 2011, *Playboy* made a further decision to sell off its TV and online services to Manwin. Instead of photographing naked models, Playboy Enterprises CEO Scott Flanders explained that the company would focus on licensing its name and logos as a brand management company. These changes in corporate structure impact one of the most globally visible brands at a time of projected steady—but not remarkable—revenue growth for the company.

What *is* remarkable is the expected increase in Internet porn use. Between 2015 and 2020, online adult viewing is expected to grow by 42 percent. An estimated 136 billion adult videos will be seen online in 2015 alone, with growth to 193 billion views by the year 2020. Viewers are increasingly turning to their phones and mobile devices. Thanks to 3G, 4G, and Wi-Fi, every global porn user around the world using a smartphone to access content was expected to watch an annual average of 348 videos as of 2015.

With such large viewership and copious amounts of uploaded content, there are signs that people who may not have previously considered working in porn are now hoping to cash in. Some crowdfunding platforms are also getting into the porn business. Asked what she sees as the future of porn, Dee Dennis, organizer of the bicoastal Catalyst Conference that highlights healthy conversations about sexuality, predicts that porn "will become more independently focused, with performers doing their own shows online."

Piggy Bank Girls seems to agree. The new crowdfunding platform enables (young, able-bodied, mostly white, and normatively thin) women to fund their own venture creating porn. The site bills itself as "the first erotic crowd funding website where girls can make their dreams come true." Although if Piggy Bank Girls' crowdfunding site is a sign of things to come, one might ask why porn continues exclusively emphasizing female bodies.

In other signs of change, Make Love Not Porn CEO Cindy Gallop hopes to make her porn site not only a chance to see naked strangers get frisky but to provide a sex education resource as well. The porn industry has long been a source of intentionally educational "how-to" films such as Nina Hartley's work with Adam and Eve, Tristan Taormino's "Expert Guide" series for Vivid, and Wicked's sex education DVDs featuring Jessica Drake. But education technology has neglected the topic of sexuality, Gallop says. She hopes to change that by first raising $2 million and then building a tech infrastructure that can host the venture. It turns out, Gallop says, that most mainstream hosts such as Amazon have fine print preventing adult content. This type of policy seems at odds with the enormous amount of content available. Yet pornography is no longer a secretive product associated with trench coats, red-light districts, or brown-paper wrapped magazines delivered by mail. It is precisely the widespread availability of porn that indirectly led to Gallop's entrée to the business.

In her popular Ted Talk, Gallop describes dating younger men, mostly those in their twenties. "When I date younger men, I have sex with younger men," Gallop announced. And what Gallop found in these encounters was that hard-core pornography had distorted the way a generation of young men understood sex, reducing their physical repertoire to rote reenactments of phallocentric choreography. This is exacerbated by the double standard by which porn is readily available but where cultures are afraid to talk about sex. Hence the need for better and explicit sex education, says Gallop.

Along with a focus on education, additional hopeful trends in pornography include a growing interest in fair-trade pornography and greater attention to content that better appeals to women.

### Will Pornography Become Fair Trade?

In today's globalized pornography market, there is transnational attention to occupational health and safety, and the ethics of pornography production, distribution, and consumption. Speaking with *Cosmopolitan* magazine, director Tristan Taormino defines fair-trade pornography as a process whereby performers are paid decent wages and they are treated with care and respect. Their consent, safety, and well-being are critical, and their contributions are valued. In other words, fair-trade porn is ethical porn.

With these factors in mind, international NGOs are stepping in to pressure producers to be accountable for their impact on human rights. Some developing countries are starting to organize sex workers into collectives and unions. In Africa, countries with sex-worker coalitions include Nigeria, Mali, Uganda, and South Africa. In Asia, India, Bangladesh, Cambodia, Hong Kong, Taiwan, and Thailand all have sex-worker organizations. An Asia Pacific Network of Sex Workers is underway; and in Europe, the Sex Worker Advocacy Network helps people organize in the Eastern, Central, and Southern regions. The Global Network for Sex Work Projects (NSWP) advocates rights-based health and social services, freedom from abuse and discrimination, and self-determination for sex workers, which includes pornography actors. The NSWP recognizes that the standard paradigms fail to fully address the human rights of sex workers, especially in regard to issues such as AIDS, trafficking, and violence against women. NSWP connects regional networks that are advocating for the rights of female, male, and transgender sex workers.

In the United Kingdom, journalist and sex educator Nichi Hodgson has launched the Ethical Porn Partnership (EPP) to challenge the idea that all pornography is automatically exploitative. The goal is to provide high-quality content while advocating for the health, welfare, and rights of those who are involved in producing pornography. EPP wants to establish widespread best practices in the industry by channeling funds "to anti-trafficking, anti-sexual violence and sex education initiatives, as well as taking an unequivocal stand on condemning child abuse imagery, and all nonconsensual sexually explicit material, such as so-called 'revenge porn.' "[1]

Trafficking and slavery in pornography's supply chains are increasingly understood as critical human rights issues. One formidable challenge to fair trade and anti-trafficking efforts is that pornography production and distribution is decentralized and hard to track. "The bottom line is we don't know where a lot of pornography is produced, by whom, and what labour laws (if any) are followed. Furthermore, the stigma still attached to sex work and the political efficacy of an abolitionist approach to pornography makes it harder for researchers to gather necessary data on global industry practices and to seek input from sex workers themselves,"[2] write Rebecca Sullivan and Alan McKee. Hopefully, this will improve in the future.

Maximum effectiveness of fair-trade efforts will require support from governmental and international NGOs to remove the stigma of sex work, say Sullivan and McKee. Otherwise, the grassroots efforts of ethical, fair-trade pornographers and sex workers could remain marginalized. As for the consumer side of the industry, Tristan Taormino insists that seeking out fair-trade porn is important. "People put their money where their politics are to support local, artisanal, and independent small businesses. If they care where their coffee came from, how it was made, and how it got to the marketplace, they buy local, organic, and fair trade."[3] By this logic, porn users need to do the same thing. Consumers need to research the directors and companies who create pornography to make sure their values and content align. And, just like people don't shoplift their organic groceries, it is ethically important to buy one's pornography, not illegally download it.

Consistent with Taormino's example, the Piggy Bank Girls also claim they are committed to fair-trade porn. As their mission statement explains, people increasingly care about the provenance and the type of manufacturing involved with creating or distributing the products they consume. In an effort to produce "fair trade porn," Piggy Bank Girls take a firm stand against sexual slavery, child pornography, the promotion of violence or abuse, or the violation of animals. The way the site works is by young women posting erotic photos to receive funding for a project or a trip or to help pay for computer repairs or to take their kitten to the vet. The Piggy Bank women who are fully funded keep 80 percent of the money paid to the site by its members. The company calls this payment a donation.

A quick look at the site reveals that the majority of participants are normatively thin and predictably posed. All of them are partially clad female bodies on display. But this certainly isn't unique to Piggy Back Girls. It is fair to say that a majority of pornography currently features heteronormative, phallocentric, and often-racist material. In other words, fair-trade financial models do not guarantee that the content is progressive. This problem has certainly not gone unnoticed. As early as the 1980s, Candida Royalle embarked on founding Femme Productions to counter what she saw as a lack of diversity in porn.

### Will Feminist Porn Become More Popular?

There are signs that a new generation of creators and consumers are continuing the effort in creating ethical porn by increasing diverse representation—specifically when it comes to feminist porn.

"Feminist porn is sex-positive, depicts sexual consent and agency, and prioritizes female pleasure," Tristan Taormino explains to *Cosmopolitan*. "Feminist porn features minorities underrepresented in mainstream porn, so you may see people of different gender identities and expressions, races, body types, or abilities. Those differences will not be fetishized or stereotyped, as some mainstream porn does (with race, for example)." Feminist porn tends to feature actual female orgasms—not faked simulacra.

Although feminist porn is beginning to gain a toehold, and maybe because of these gains, there is defensiveness from some within the industry. At the 2014 AVN Adult Entertainment Expo and AVN Awards in Las Vegas, *Adult Video News* hosted a panel titled "The Feminist Porn Technique," in part to capitalize on the trend and apparently also to provide a forum for debate. Participants defined feminist porn production as being more focused on sexual agency, erotic authenticity, and diverse body types. But adult performer Stormy Daniels, who was a member of the panel, interjected—without (a) noting the irony of her statement and (b) mistakenly assuming that one needs certain genitalia to be a feminist—that her "vagina has nothing to do with porn." This prompted sexuality scholar Lynn

Comella to tweet from the audience: "Stormy Daniels says she's not comfortable with the label 'feminist porn' *during* the feminist porn panel. (Awkward?) #AVN #AEE #AEExpo."

Writing for the blog *Ms. Naughty's Porn for Women*, adult filmmaker Louise Lush wrote that with feminist porn hitting the mainstream industry, some people were getting uncomfortable. "People are getting offended by the idea of 'feminist porn' because it's making them think critically about porn in general," says Lush.

Stormy Daniels is not alone in misunderstanding the meaning of feminist porn. Speaking to this issue, Erika Lust, author of *Good Porn: A Woman's Guide*, describes her foray into producing adult content. Uneasy about increasing violence in mainstream pornography and interested in more cinematic films about sex, Lust began crowdsourcing plot ideas for porn movies of her own. For Lust, making ethical porn means "the sex can stay dirty, but the values have to be clean." Yet, Erika Lust hesitates to use the term "feminist porn" in describing her work because although 60 percent of her audience is men, there is a persistent assumption that feminist porn is women's-only porn.

However, this is a misreading of the situation. Feminist porn is not exclusively for or about women and femininity. "In lots of mainstream porn, men are portrayed as one-dimensional sex robots; they are always dominant, assertive, and rock hard. In a lot of films, we rarely get to see men's faces or the rest of their bodies. They are reduced to merely disembodied penises," says Taormino.[4] Feminist pornography instead uses aesthetics and filmmaking styles that empower the performers who make it and the people who watch it. In exploring ideas about desire, beauty, pleasure, and power, feminist porn shows men who get off on giving pleasure, straight men who get anally penetrated, and men who aren't afraid to challenge the norms of hegemonic masculinity. Queer performer Ned Henry (né Mayhem) describes his experience in front of the camera, commenting that the male body is rarely displayed for aesthetic and erotic pleasure in straight porn. Gay porn is obviously made for homosexual male arousal, and the male body is meant to be the visual trigger. But "most mainstream porn is made for a heterosexual male gaze. Female bodies are the currency of arousal, and male performers are usually headless stunt cocks.... The assumption is that it would make the (male) audience uncomfortable to sexualize a man's body."[5] People creating and watching feminist pornography hope to change that.

Heterosexual men are rarely thought of as visually arousing, and people assume women are not visually aroused. "I call bullshit," says Henry. There is something fun and empowering about *consensual* objectification, he continues. "Portraying masculinity and queerness in porn in new ways can help change the cultural weight of these identities" and assumptions. "A growing number of pornographers share similar mission statements, and I hope that as a result fewer people will feel personally judged when they look for sexy images on the Internet,"[6] Henry comments.

### Will More Porn Be Made for Women?

In addition to misreading about feminist porn, there is a misunderstanding that porn made for women amounts to *Fifty Shades of Grey*. This book series, which has been accused of being "50 shades of abuse," garnered its author E.L. James $95 million, making her the world's highest earning writer. Porn for women goes far beyond *50 Shades*, but neither is it vanilla sex filled with rose petals, violins, and soft lens focus. There is a stereotype that women want kinder, gentler, romantic porn. Some women do, and some women don't. Many women want to explore sexual power dynamics in a "explicitly consensual and more diverse, nuanced, non-stereotypical way," Taormino continues. Erika Lust's porn film venture, XConfessions, reveals just how explicit women want their porn to be with titles such as "I Pegged My Boyfriend" and an array of fetish sidelines for sale.

Asked during an online Reddit forum (known as "Ask Me Anything") whether she feels an obligation to disprove people's perspective that porn objectifies women, director Shine Louise Houston replies that pornography has been made a scapegoat for cultural hang-ups about sex and sexuality. "We have movies that make us laugh or cry or excite us through explosions ... but when we have stories about sex, people get antsy." Some people are never going to like porn, says Houston, just like she is averse to slasher movies. However, the answer is not to censor pornography. We need positive images of sex in all its variety, says Houston. "Sex is one of the funniest, most awkward, and beautiful things that humans do. Also if there were documentaries and articles that wrote about the industry the way it really works and how diverse it is there would be less opportunity to dump all of our issues onto porn as the big bad problem with society today."[7]

### What Is Queer Porn?

In contrast with the practice of blaming porn for all of society's problematic social norms, there is a long history of feminist, queer, and lesbian porn performers creating content to instead shift the social norms of the genre. In the "Golden Age of Porn," Candida Royalle, along with Veronica Hart, Gloria Leonard, and Veronica Vera, recognized there was a market for sex-positive films. Lesbian porn for dykes and femmes was an untapped market when Debi Sundhal, Nan Kinney, Susie Bright, Shar Rednour, and Jacki Strano launched *On Our Backs* and SIR Video in the 1980s and 1990s, respectively. As the famous porn performer and artist Annie Sprinkle said, "The answer to bad porn isn't no porn ... it's to try and make better porn!" Queer porn and nonracist porn ventures seek to do exactly what Annie Sprinkle suggested.

Award-winning genderqueer porn performer Jiz Lee explains the relatively recent development of queer porn.[8] The term was coined around the mid-1990s through companies

NoFauxxx.com and CrashPadSeries.com; the porn includes a mix of queer gender identities in a given film or episode. Any number of expressions can be present including transwomen, transmen, cisgender women, cisgender men, dyke couples, gay couples, bisexuals, femmes, butches, genderqueer people, and many more.

The emphasis in queer porn is authentic desire and sexual representation; thus there tends to be diversity in body size, abilities, sex acts, kink, people of color, as well as the level of performers' experience—meaning there is professional and amateur crossover. In addition to Shine Louise Houston, other directors in the genre include Courtney Trouble and Madison Young, who has created a name for queer and bisexual performers. The late Carlos Batts was a queer-friendly director who, with his wife and muse April Flores, created artistically compelling films that are also diverse in size and ethnicities. Their final project before Carlos Batts's untimely passing was the book titled *Fat Girl*, featuring photographic images of April Flores throughout.

There are queer-friendly distribution companies such as Good Releasing, a sister company of Good Vibrations in San Francisco. There are also Canadian companies and directors involved in the queer porn movement that include Bren Ryder of Vancouver. The Toronto sex toy company Good For Her produces the annual Feminist Porn Awards, which honored both Jiz Lee and Buck Angel with Boundary Breakers awards. Among transwomen creating pornography, Tobi Hill-Meyer produced "Doing it For Ourselves: the Transwoman Porn Project." The porn documentary *Trans Entities*, by director Morty Diamond, features genderqueer performer Papi Coxxx and includes discussions on polyamory, gender identity, kink and role-playing, and negotiating relationships with a deaf lover. Also part of what Jiz Lee calls "the queer porn family" is Trannywood Pictures, which aims to normalize transsexual men within the gay community and to also advocate and portray safer sex practices.

FurryGirl and Tasty Tricksie, Ms. Naughty, and Sophia St. James are independent camera models and female directors who have been active in online discussions around sex work and independent pornography.

Established director/performers Belladonna and Joanna Angel have done a form of crossover work involving San Francisco's indie porn cinema and the L.A. production-style shoots. Other performers who shoot for both mainstream and indie in this way include Syd Blakovich and Dylan Ryan, as well as Lorelei Lee and Princess Donna, who are also very well known in fetish niches such as Kink.com. There are also cisgender male performers who have had interesting experiences performing in straight/gay/queer porn such as Wolf Hudson, Danny Wylde, and Mickey Mod. Shine Louise Houston is perhaps the only female director to run a gay male website (heavenlyspire.com), which explores the masculine sexualities of cisgender and transmen equally. As Jiz Lee implies, this history reveals the links between queer pornography and the politics of sexual liberation. And, with such well-developed foundations, there are indications that queer porn will continue to grow in the future.

Although not exclusively queer, Seattle's annual HUMP! festival also evokes the spirit of sexual liberation and is certainly queer friendly. In existence since 2005, HUMP! features authentically "homegrown" submissions from everyday people who want to make porn. The festival picks the best submissions including "the funniest, sweetest, kinkiest, and most hardcore. The entries are straight, gay, lesbian, bi, trans, and genderqueer. Almost all of the films have plots and every one of them is sex-positive," wrote Kelly O for Seattle's local weekly, *The Stranger*. Every year, all copies of the films are destroyed once they are screened. And, making HUMP! unique in a digital era that promotes isolation, the films are shown in real theaters, requiring people to sit next to other people in an audience, and without fast-forwarding.

## *Will Pornography Be Taught in College?*

Pornography is among the most used products but least taught topics on a college campus. That said, pornography is now included in courses across the country at campuses such as Spelman College, Indiana University, Texas A&M, Rutgers, and the University of Pennsylvania. These courses go by titles such as Sexual Economies, Sexuality and Race, Hip Hop Feminism, and The Politics of Pornography. They are taught in a range of departments including political science, gender studies, and communications. These classes include a diverse emphasis including labor and public policy issues, public health, sexual politics, and the law.

Among the earliest to teach the material, film scholar Constance Penley, who has taught courses on pornography at the University of California, Santa Barbara, since the 1990s, explains that porn is "a genre of film and media that has been central to the development of technology, culture, and society over the last one hundred years."

In 1993, Penley suggested to her colleagues that although their university was lauded for having one of the foremost media and film programs, they neglected to teach "the most enduring and prolific of genres." Faculty agreed that to remain among the strongest academic leaders in film and media studies, they needed to include pornography in the curriculum.[9] Yet where scholars in other academic fields are expected to have extensive expertise and breadth and depth of knowledge, pornography may be more easily discounted as a legitimate area of expertise, as relevant as it may be to psychology, politics, sociology, or any number of fields.[10]

Like other professors who teach about pornography, Penley's courses are contextualized in her field of expertise. For the most part, Penley's students are advanced film and media majors. These students analyze pornography by asking the same questions they normally ask about other forms of film, such as how the camera styles and content has changed over time, or questions about the legal climate and its impact on modes of production, consumption, and distribution. "As a society, we debate, legislate, regulate pornography in almost a total vacuum of knowledge about what it really consists of historically, textually, institutionally. I tell my students," Penley says, "that they can have their opinions, but only after they know what pornography is."[11]

Although Penley initially intended to teach a university pornography course in the context of film history, her first run of this course inadvertently became a class on sex education. This, Penley explains, was due, in no small part, to the dismal sex education provided to students before they arrive at college. "In one of my first pornography courses," Penley recounts, "I recall watching an anal sex scene for the first time in the class. I was sitting next to one of my students and she whispered to herself, 'I didn't know you could do that.' "[12]

Because pornography is often a source of information about sexuality, this provides all the more reason to consider the importance of teaching pornography and of developing ethical pedagogy. Although teaching porn literacy may be delegitimized or perceived as a risky venture, the subject can be an important conduit for discussing consumer culture, democracy, disagreement, and free speech. This does not necessarily mean defending pornography but rather "to show its diversity, complexity, and historicity ... and to educate students about pornography as a popular field of representation and a political economy informed by gender, race, class, and culture."[13] Taught well, college-level pornography courses promote stronger abilities to navigate sexual and gender politics. Porn can be a source of sexual pleasure or a subject of prurient interest, but it is also an important media genre for questioning normative expectations and exploring forms of resistance that challenge racism, classism, ageism, and related intersectional subjugations.

The growing tradition of porn education includes documentary films, slide shows, and video compilation road shows dating back several decades. These encompass a range of political and ideological perspectives. Among these are Bonnie Sherr

Klein's documentary, "Not a Love Story" (1982); Susie Bright's feminist pro-sex films, "How to Read a Dirty Movie" and "All Girl Action: The History of Lesbian Eroticism in Hollywood" (1987); Focus on the Family's reactionary "Learn to Discern" (1992); Gail Dines's conservative feminist project, "Who Wants to be a Pornstar?" (2007); and the many new books, blogs, and journals on the subject.

As a sign of pornography's increasing academic legitimacy, the journal *Porn Studies* launched in 2014. One year prior to this launch, an international petition was organized to oppose the perceived "pro porn" bias of the journal and demand that its publisher, Routledge, stop publication. The petition was sponsored by Stop Porn Culture and signed by an array of activists and academics. Soon after the anti-*Porn Studies* petition was circulated, Sage Publications announced it would begin publishing *Sexualization, Media & Society*. This new journal's editorial board includes several anti-pornography scholars—many of whom signed the petition—and features articles exploring the social, behavioral, cultural, and health effects of Internet pornography (and other forms of hypersexualized media).

### How Might Technology Change Pornography?

Based on the close relationship between technology and pornography in the past, it is reasonable to guess they will remain tethered in the future. What is less clear is which technologies will emerge as the frontrunners.

Google Glass is a wearable technology that looks like eyeglasses and contains what the company calls an optical head-mounted display. Google Glass would enable the wearer to access the Internet using voice commands. Google announced in 2013 that it was banning adult content from Google Glass, and then announced in 2015 that they were stopping production of the prototype.

At around this time, *Xbiz* announced "Ready or Not, Virtual Reality Is Now Steamrolling Its Way into the Adult

Entertainment Industry." The porn industry has long been among the early adopters of new technology and virtual reality (VR) is consistent with this pattern. VR is an immersive experience that puts the user in the center of the visual and auditory action. As one company getting on board early, the adult movie streaming service provider SugarDVD announced they were developing an interactive technology in which users could "choose their own adventure," with alternative endings much like the technology available to online gamers.

Some caution, however, that all the exciting technology in the universe won't make up for lackluster content. Writing for *Fortune*, Erika Lust opines that without fresh perspectives and storylines, VR technology simply "creates the same repetitive, boring adult content we've seen for years. It's still just mechanical sex made by men, for men: gynecological shots, fake orgasms, tacky costumes and settings and zero narrative." No heat, no passion, no context, says Lust, who explains that based on what she's seen so far in VR clips or scenes, "we are still far from a transformative and enjoyable experience."[14]

Tech pundits predict that with or without fresh content, VR is going to be a big flop. Along with it, virtual porn would presumably also go limp. For one thing, the "fisheye" effect hampers many of the 360-degree views depicted by current VR systems. This distorts straight lines into curved images, which might work fine for virtual real estate walk-throughs or even outdoor nature scenes, but just looks weird when it comes to making human bodies look sexy. There is also a question about whether VR might be distracting given the amount of visual background detail it includes.

Finally, there is the price. As of 2015, Oculus CEO Brian Iribe estimated that a brand new PC and an Oculus VR would cost $1,500. If a customer needs to update their graphics card, the cost for an upgrade and a headset would be roughly $1,000. The ability to run on a Mac, tablets, or smartphones remains in the future. If VR succeeds, its major stakeholders stand to benefit enormously, including Google, Microsoft, and Facebook-owned Oculus.

## What about Porn in Space?

If Pornhub has its way, it will be the first adult company to film sex in space. Given the industry's penchant for playful video titles combined with Pornub's history of providing access to stolen porn, perhaps their venture will be called Pirates in Space. Tech.mic reported that Pornhub was teaming up with adult studio Digital Playground in attempting to raise $3.4 million to send two porn performers into space to film a sex tape. About $2 million will go to buying room on a commercial spaceflight and for the six months to train actors Eva Lovia and Johnny Sin how to be temporary astronauts. The financially and technologically ambitious Indiegogo campaign fell short of its goal, but the concept for "interstellar nookie" is attention getting and not entirely unlikely in the future. Scientists warn, however, that sex in space can be difficult given physiological changes to heart rate and arousal and the fact that every push or thrust in space propels the astronaut in the opposite direction.

## Will People Ever Stop Fighting about Porn?

By the time there is porn in space, there will hopefully also be enough reliable data and clear philosophy to put to rest the fights about whether pornography causes violence, whether it is ethical, and whether new technology will turn us into what Erika Lust calls "porn-consuming zombie junkies."

But these debates have been going on for years. In the 1980s, findings by the Meese Commission, radical feminists, and Christian conservatives aligned in opposing pornography. Free speech arguments, "pro-sex" feminists, and some of the raunchiest misogynist pornographers continue making similar arguments in protecting the First Amendment and promoting sexually libertine agendas. As the saying goes, politics makes strange bedfellows. Some might suggest that if you find your bedfellows are strange, you might want to reconsider the politics that led you to cozy up in that inelegant way.

But this is a challenging dilemma. What's more, describing a piece of porn—even to critique it—is to produce a piece of porn, as philosopher Nancy Bauer points out. Ronald Reagan's Meese Commission did this, as did anti-pornography feminist Andrea Dworkin. Members of Stop Porn Culture, who worry that pornographic images will exist without consent and in perpetuity on the Internet, overlook the fact that they use these same porn images, without consent from the performers, in creating their anti-porn slide shows and public lectures.

Pornography is a lightning rod for opinions about sexual health and morality, and for an exquisitely political question: *how can we both recognize human agency while acknowledging the constraints of life?* Despite some measure of progressive change among industry practices, there remain concerns about violence, extreme content, human rights, and liberation. It's worth pausing to note that pornography has been around for as long as visual images and the written word have existed; and yet the debates about pornography have, for so long, remained stagnant. There is the anti-porn cohort who is angry at the anti-anti porn contingency (yes, that is a thing), and a pro-porn alliance that seems at times to gloss over legitimate concerns about the industry. The free speech advocates battle conservative moralists in a fight that boils down to *Is porn good?* or *Is porn bad?* Neither position yields a whole lot of insight.

As we move into the future, the debates about pornography—and all that it represents—will undoubtedly continue. The good news is it looks like we are beginning to move beyond unproductive, binary stalemates. The issue of pornography embodies quite literally questions about sexual delight and subjugation, liberation and constraint. Pornography evokes inspiration for exploration, expression . . . and can provoke repression, apathy, and destruction as well. If we are going to advocate successfully for a safe and ethical world, if we care about gender justice, and if we are devoted to more fully understanding the politics of pleasure and danger, then moving past the porn wars is a welcome requirement for the future.

# NOTES

## Chapter 1

1. B. Ruby Rich, "Anti-Porn: Soft Issue, Hard World," *Feminist Review* 13 (Spring 1983): 60.
2. Joseph W. Slade, *Pornography in America* (Santa Barbara: Praeger, 2000), 3.
3. Caroline Heldman and Lisa Wade, "A Call for a Twenty-First Century 'Sex Wars,'" (paper presented at the annual meeting of the Western Political Science Association, Los Angeles, March 28, 2013), 6.

## Chapter 2

1. Kevin Heffernan, "Seen as a Business: Adult Film's Historical Framework and Foundations," in *New Views on Pornography: Sexuality, Politics, and the Law*, ed. Lynn Comella and Shira Tarrant (Santa Barbara, CA: Praeger, 2015), 37–56.
2. Joseph W. Slade, "Eroticism and Technological Regression: The Stag Film," *History and Technology* 22, no. 1 (March 2006): 28.
3. Stephanie Pappas, "The History of Pornography No More Prudish Than the Present," *Live Science*, October 11, 2010, http://www.livescience.com/8748-history-pornography-prudish-present.html.

## Chapter 3

1. Ned Mayhem, "Male and Queer in the Porn Industry," in *Men Speak Out: Views on Gender, Sex, and Power*, 2nd ed., ed. Shira Tarrant (New York: Routledge, 2013), 85.

2. Lynsey G, "Blowing the Budget: Feminist Porn Start-Ups Are Getting Spanked When It Comes to Finances," *Bitch* 64 (Fall 2014): 45.

3. Danny Wylde, *SWAAY*, http://www.swaay.org/porn.html.

4. Stephanie Pappas, "The History of Pornography No More Prudish Than the Present," *Live Science*, October 11, 2010, http://www.livescience.com/8748-history-pornography-prudish-present.html.

5. Sam Schechner and Jessica E. Vascellaro, "TV Porn Doesn't Sell Like It Used To," *The Wall Street Journal*, August 5, 2011, http://www.wsj.com/articles/SB10001424053111903885604576488540447354036.

6. Lee Quarnstrom, email message to the author, May 15, 2015.

7. Gail Dines, email message to wmst-L@Listserv.umd.edu, February 29, 2012, 3:32 pm.

8. Nate Gates, "Takedown Piracy Presents Game Changer in Fight Against Piracy," *Takedown Piracy*, November 10, 2014, http://takedownpiracy.com/2014/11/takedown-piracy-presents-game-changer-in-fight-against-piracy/.

9. EJ Dickson, "Pornhub Makes a Splash at the AVNs, the Oscars for Adult Entertainment," *Daily Dot*, January 29, 2015, http://dailydot.com/lifestyle/pornhub-controversy-avn-awards.

## Chapter 4

1. Stoya, "What Porn Actors Don't Talk About," *New Statesman*, June 1, 2015, http://www.newstatesman.com/2015/05/what-porn-actors-don-t-talk-about.

2. Aurora Snow, "The Adult Industry Doesn't Pay! (As Much As You Think)," *The Daily Beast*, November 23, 2013, http://www.thedailybeast.com/articles/2013/11/23/the-adult-industry-doesn-t-pay-as-much-as-you-think.html.

3. Tracy Clark-Flory, "Keeping It Up in the Porn Industry," *The Fix*, September 30, 2014, http://www.thefix.com/content/keeping-it-porn-industry.

4. Nina Hartley, "Porn: An Effective Vehicle for Sexual Role Modeling and Education," in *The Feminist Porn Book: The Politics of Producing Pleasure*, ed. Tristan Taormino et al. (New York: The Feminist Press, 2013), 228.

5. Caitlin Cruz, "The Deep Class Issues Hidden in Explosive New Doc About Amateur Porn," *Talking Points Memo*, June 3, 2015,

http://talkingpointsmemo.com/cafe/class-issues-missing-from-hot-girls-wanted.

6. Gail Dines, *Pornland: How Porn Has Hijacked our Sexuality* (Boston: Beacon Press, 2010), xxvii–xxviii.

7. Chris Nieratko, "Catching Up with the Actress Formerly Known as Belladonna," *Vice*, January 9, 2015, http://www.vice.com/en_ca/read/catching-up-with-the-actress-formerly-known-as-belladonna-000.

8. Susannah Breslin, "The Hardest Thing About Being a Male Porn Star," *Forbes.com*, April 23, 2012, http://www.forbes.com/sites/susannahbreslin/2012/04/23/the-hardest-thing-about-being-a-male-porn-star/.

## Chapter 5

1. Quoted in Martha McCaughey, *The Caveman Mystique: Pop-Darwinism and the Debates Over Sex, Violence, and Science* (New York: Routledge, 2008), 72.

2. CBS News, *CBS Money Watch*, "SEC Staffers Watched Porn as Economy Crashed," April 22, 2010, http://www.cbsnews.com/news/sec-staffers-watched-porn-as-economy-crashed/.

3. Jason S. Carroll, Laura M. Padilla-Walker, Larry J. Nelson, Chad D. Olson, Carolyn McNamara Barry, and Stephanie D. Madsen, "Generation XXX: Pornography Acceptance and Use Among Emerging Adults," *Journal of Adolescent Research* 23, no. 1 (January 2008): 6–30.

4. Clarissa Smith, Martin Barker, and Feona Attwood, "Why Do People Use Porn? Results From PornResearch.org," in *New Views on Pornography: Sexuality, Politics, and the Law*, ed. Lynn Comella and Shira Tarrant (Santa Barbara, CA: Praeger, 2015), 277–296.

5. Ibid., 283–284.

6. Kristian Danebac, Bente Træen, and Sven-Axel Månsson, "Use of Pornography in a Random Sample of Norwegian Heterosexual Couples," *Archives of Sexual Behavior* 38, no. 5 (2009): 752.

7. Cara C. MacInnis and Gordon Hodson, "Do American States With More Religious or Conservative Populations Search More for Sexual Content on Google?" *Archives of Sexual Behavior* 44, no. 1 (2015): 145, 146.

8. http://www.pornmd.com/live-search

9. Ronald Weitzer, "Interpreting the Data: Assessing Competing Claims in Pornography Research," in *New Views on Pornography: Sexuality, Politics, and the Law*, ed. Lynn Comella and Shira Tarrant (Santa Barbara, CA: Praeger, 2015), 259.

10. Andy Ruddock, "Pornography and Effects Studies: What Does the Research Actually Say?" in *New Views on Pornography: Sexuality, Politics, and the Law*, ed. Lynn Comella and Shira Tarrant (Santa Barbara, CA: Praeger, 2015), 297–318.

11. Kristen Purcell, "Online Video 2013," Pew Research Center's Internet & American Life Project, October 10, 2013, 10.

12. Denver Nicks, "12 Percent of Americans Admit to Watching Porn Online, the Other 88 Percent Must Not Have Internet," *Time*, October 3, 2013, http://newsfeed.time.com/2013/10/10/12-percent-of-americans-admit-to-watching-porn-online-the-other-88-percent-must-not-have-internet/.

### Chapter 6

1. Gail Dines, "Stop Porn Culture: Those Who Watch Modern Porn Are Becoming Increasingly Desensitised," *The Independent*, March 17, 2014, http://www.independent.co.uk/voices/comment/stop-porn-culture-those-who-watch-modern-porn-are-becoming-increasingly-desensitised-9195395.html.

2. Alana Massey, "Porn Is Not Coming for Our Sex Lives," *Pacific Standard,* April 3, 2015, http://www.psmag.com/books-and-culture/its-all-ok-you-can-watch-some-porn-right-after-you-read-this-article.

3. Ana J. Bridges et al., "Aggression and Sexual Behavior in Best-Selling Pornography Videos: A Content Analysis Update," *Violence Against Women* 16 (October 2010): 1065–1085.

4. Marleen J. E. Klaassen and Jochen Peter, "Gender (In)equality in Internet Pornography: A Content Analysis of Popular Pornographic Internet Videos," *The Journal of Sex Research*, November 24, 2014, http://www.tandfonline.com/doi/full/10.1080/00224499.2014.976781#abstract.

5. Carole Cadwalladr, "Porn Wars: The Debate That's Dividing Academia," *The Guardian*, June 15, 2013, http://www.theguardian.com/culture/2013/jun/16/internet-violent-porn-crime-studies.

6. Ronald Weitzer, "Pornography: Popular Claims vs. the Evidence" in *New Views on Pornography: Sexuality, Politics, and the Law*, ed.

Lynn Comella and Shira Tarrant (Santa Barbara, CA: Praeger, 2015), 258.

7. Vivian Dent and Michael Bader, "Is Pornography Really Harmful?" *AlterNet*, Sex and Relationships, November 6, 2007, http://www.alternet.org/sex/67144/?page=1.

8. "Are the Effects of Pornography Negligible?" University of Montreal Press Release, December 1, 2009, http://www.eurekalert.org/pub_releases/2009-12/uom-ate120109.php.

9. Anna Pulley, "What Happened at My First Porn Shoot," *AlterNet*, October 20, 2011, http://www.alternet.org/story/152804/what_happened_at_my_first_porn_shoot.

10. Mireille Miller-Young, *A Taste for Brown Sugar: Black Women in Pornography* (Durham, NC: Duke University Press, 2014), ix–xi.

11. Mireille Miller-Young, "Race and the Politics of Agency in Porn: A Conversation with Black BBW Performer Betty Blac," in *New Views on Pornography: Sexuality, Politics, and the Law*, ed. Lynn Comella and Shira Tarrant (Santa Barbara, CA: Praeger, 2015), 360.

12. Antoine Mazières et al., "Deep Tags: Toward a Quantitative Analysis of Online Pornography," *Porn Studies* 1, no. 1–2 (2014): 92.

13. Patrick A. Trueman, "Porn Creates Demand for Sex Trafficking," *Miami Herald*, op-ed, July 23, 2014, http://www.miamiherald.com/2014/07/23/4251372/porn-creates-demand-for-sex-trafficking.html.

14. *The Economist*, "The Sex Industry: Giving the Customer What He Wants," February 14 (1998): 21–23.

15. Quoted in Patrick A. Trueman, "Porn Creates Demand for Sex Trafficking," *Miami Herald*, op-ed, July 23, 2014, http://www.miamiherald.com/2014/07/23/4251372/porn-creates-demand-for-sex-trafficking.html.

16. Rebecca Sullivan and Alan McKee, *Pornography: Structures, Agency and Performance* (Cambridge, UK: Polity, 2015).

17. Justin Lehmiller, "Is Pornography Harmful to Our Brains and to Our Love Lives?," *Sex and Psychology*, March 19, 2012, http://www.lehmiller.com/blog/2012/3/19/is-pornography-harmful-to-our-brains-and-to-our-love-lives.html?rq=pornography.

18. Constance Penley, "'A Feminist Teaching Pornography? That's Like Scopes Teaching Evolution!'" in *The Feminist Porn Book: The Politics of Producing Pleasure*, ed. Tristan Taormino et al. (New York: The Feminist Press, 2013), 187.

19. Clarissa Smith, Martin Barker, and Feona Attwood, "Why Do People Watch Porn? Results from PornResearch.Org," in *New Views on Pornography: Sexuality, Politics, and the Law*, ed. Lynn Comella and Shira Tarrant (Santa Barbara, CA: Praeger, 2015), 277–296.

## Chapter 7

1. Kimberly A. Harchuck, "Pornography and the First Amendment Right to Free Speech," in *New Views on Pornography: Sexuality, Politics, and the Law*, ed. Lynn Comella and Shira Tarrant (Santa Barbara, CA: Praeger, 2015), 15.
2. The following definition is documented in Winifred Ann Sandler, "The Minneapolis Anti-Pornography Ordinance: A Valid Assertion of Civil Rights?" *Fordham Urban Law Journal* 13, no. 4 (1984): 912.
3. Nadine Strossen, *Defending Pornography: Free Speech, Sex, and the Fight for Women's Rights* (New York: New York University Press, 2000), 75–79.
4. Susannah Breslin, "To the Max," November 7, 2013, http://susannahbreslin.net/blog/2013/11/7/to-the-max.
5. Ibid.
6. Jerry Barnett, "The British Porn Industry's Ambiguity Towards Opposing Censorship," *Porn Studies* 1, no. 3 (2014): 321–325.
7. Frankie Mullen, "British BDSM Enthusiasts, Say Goodbye to Your Favourite Homegrown Porn," *Vice*, December 1, 2014, http://www.vice.com/en_uk/read/the-end-of-uk-bdsm-282.
8. Kayla Webley, "The Best Revenge: California's Top Cop Kamala Harris Is Leading the Charge Against 'Revenge Porn,'" *Marie Claire*, July 2015, 65.

## Chapter 8

1. Free Speech Coalition, "FSC Responds to Complaint Filed by AHF Against Immoral Productions," March 19, 2013, http://freespeechcoalition.com/fsc-responds-to-complaint-filed-by-ahf-against-immoral-productions/.
2. James Nye, "Tearful HIV Positive Porn Star Lovers Appear Together at Emotional Press Conference to Hit Out at Insufficient Testing Within the Industry," *Daily Mail*, September 18, 2013, http://www.dailymail.co.uk/news/article-2424664/Porn-industry-HIV-outbreak-HIV-positive-porn-stars-say-testing-14-days-NOT-enough.html.

3. Elizabeth Cohen, "Porn Producer Vows to Mandate Condoms After HIV Scare," *CNN*, September 20, 2013, http://www.cnn.com/2013/09/20/health/porn-industry-condoms-hiv/index.html.

4. Tracy Clark-Flory, "Porn Star Madison Young: Making 'Safe' Sexy," *Salon*, October 18, 2010, http://www.salon.com/2010/10/18/madison_young/.

5. Meeting Minutes, "Bloodborne Pathogens in the Adult Film Industry," Cal/OSHA Advisory Meeting, June 29, 2010, http://www.dir.ca.gov/dosh/DoshReg/meeting_minutes_6-29-10.pdf, 3.

6. John Sanford, "Adult Industry Contingent Opposes Cal/OSHA Regs at San Diego Hearing," *Xbiz*, May 21, 2015, http://newswire.xbiz.com/view.php?id=194856.

7. "HIV Scare in US Porn Industry After Two Actors Test Positive," *The Guardian*, December 31, 2014, http://www.theguardian.com/us-news/2014/dec/31/hiv-scare-porn-actors-positive-nevada.

8. Rowenna Davis, "Labiaplasty Surgery Increase Blamed on Pornography," *The Guardian*, February 26, 2011, http://www.theguardian.com/lifeandstyle/2011/feb/27/labiaplasty-surgery-labia-vagina-pornography?INTCMP=SRCH.

9. Bethany Jones and Camille Nurka, "Labiaplasty and Pornography: A Preliminary Investigation," *Porn Studies* 2, no. 1 (2015): 62.

10. *SWAAY: Sex Work Activists, Allies, and You*, 2011, http://www.swaay.org/porn.html.

11. C. Marsten and R. Lewis, "Anal Heterosex Among Young People and Implications for Health Promotion: A Qualitative Study in the UK," *BMJ Open 2014*, http://bmjopen.bmj.com/content/4/8/e004996.full.

12. Michael Flood, "Young Men Using Pornography," in *Everyday Pornography*, ed. Karen Boyle (New York: Routledge, 2010), 173.

## Chapter 9

1. Seth Lubove, "Sex, Lies and Statistics," *Forbes*, November 23, 2005, http://www.forbes.com/2005/11/22/internet-pornography-children-cz_sl_1123internet.html.

2. Michele L. Ybarra and Kimberly Mitchell, "Exposure to Internet Pornography among Children and Adolescents: A National Survey," *Cyberpsychology & Behavior* 8, no. 5 (2005): 473–486, http://

unh.edu/ccrc/pdf/jvq/CV76.pdf. This data does not account for unwanted exposure to pornography among teens.

3. Heather Saul, "Porn Seen By a Quarter of Children Under 12, Survey Finds," *The Independent*, April 10, 2014, http://www.independent.co.uk/arts-entertainment/tv/news/porn-seen-by-a-quarter-of-children-under-12-survey-finds-9251019.html.

4. Quoted by Mark Pattison, Catholic News Service, "Research Details Pornography's Harmful Effects to Women, Society," *National Catholic Reporter*, May 21, 2014, http://ncronline.org/news/accountability/research-details-pornographys-harmful-effects-women-society.

5. Bella English, "The Secret Life of Boys: Pornography Is Just a Mouse Click Away, and Kids Are Being Exposed to It in Ever-Increasing Numbers," *The Boston Globe*, May 12, 2005, D1.

6. Quoted by Rick Nauert, "Pornography's Effect on Men Under Study," *PsychCentral*, http://psychcentral.com/news/2009/12/02/pornographys-effect-on-men-under-study/9884.html.

7. Public Release, "Are the Effects of Porn Negligible?," *EurekAlert! The Global Source for Science News*, December 1, 2009, http://www.eurekalert.org/pub_releases/2009-12/uom-ate120109.php.

8. Michael Flood, "The Harms of Pornography Exposure Among Children and Young People," *Child Abuse Review* 18 (2009): 384–400.

9. Robert Weiss, "What Is Online Pornography Doing to Our Boys?" *HuffPost Healthy Living*, September 25, 2015, http://www.huffingtonpost.com/robert-weiss/what-is-online-pornograph_b_5881782.html.

10. Todd Melby, "Teens, Porn and the Digital Age," *Contemporary Sexuality* 44, no. 9 (September 2010): 5.

11. Miranda A. H. Horvath et al., "'Basically ... Porn Is Everywhere': A Rapid Evidence Assessment on the Effects that Access and Exposure to Pornography Has on Children and Young People," Office of the Children's Commissioner/Middlesex University London (2013): 7, http://www.mdx.ac.uk/__data/assets/pdf_file/0008/58148/BasicallyporniseverywhereReport.pdf.

12. Peggy Drexler, "How Much Porn Is Your Kid Watching?" *The Daily Beast*, October 4, 2013, http://www.thedailybeast.com/witw/articles/2013/10/04/how-much-porn-is-your-kid-watching.html.

13. Christian Graugaard quoted in Arielle Pardes, "What We Talk About When We Talk About Porn," *Vice*, March 20, 2015, http://www.vice.com/read/what-we-talk-about-when-we-talk-about-porn-320.

14. Chanel Darcey, "Porn Becoming Substitute for Sex Education," *WAToday*, July 22, 2013, http://www.watoday.com.au/wa-news/ porn-becoming-substitute-for-sex-education-20130721-2q9e7.

15. Shira Tarrant, "Pornography 101: Why College Kids Need Porn Literacy Training," *AlterNet*, September 15, 2010, http://www. alternet.org/story/148129/pornography_101%3A_why_college_ kids_need_porn_literacy_training.

16. Michael Flood, "The Harms of Pornography Exposure Among Children and Young People," *Child Abuse Review* 18 (2009): 394.

17. Helen Russell, "Porn Belongs in the Classroom, Says Danish Professor," *The Guardian*, March 15, 2015, http://www. theguardian.com/culture/2015/mar/16/pornography- belongs-classroom-professor-denmark.

18. David Segal, "Does Porn Hurt Children?," *New York Times*, March 28, 2014, http://www.nytimes.com/2014/03/29/sunday-review/ does-porn-hurt-children.html?emc=edit_th_20140330&nl=today sheadlines&nlid=25366898&_r=2.

19. Natasha Culzac, "Anal Sex Study Reveals Climate of 'Coercion,'" *The Independent*, August 15, 2015, http://www.independent.co.uk/ life-style/health-and-families/health-news/women-being- coerced-into-having-anal-sex-researchers-say-with-persuasion- normalised-9671395.html.

20. Abby Young-Powell, "Students Turn to Porn for Sex Education," *The Guardian*, January 29, 2015, http://www.theguardian.com/ education/2015/jan/29/students-turn-to-porn-for-sex-education.

### Chapter 10

1. "Ethical Porn Partnership," on Nichi Hodgson's website, http:// nichihodgson.com/ethical-porn-partnership/.

2. Rebecca Sullivan and Alan McKee, *Pornography: Structures, Agency and Performance* (Cambridge, UK: Polity, 2015).

3. Anna Breslaw, "So, What *Is* Feminist Porn? Find Out From a Woman Who Makes It," *Cosmopolitan*, November 6, 2013, http://www.cosmopolitan.com/sex-love/news/a16343/tristan- taormino-feminist-porn-interview/.

4. Ibid.

5. Ned Mayhem, "Male and Queer in the Porn Industry," in *Men Speak Out: Views on Gender, Sex, and Power*, ed. Shira Tarrant (New York: Routledge, 2013), 82–83.

6. Ibid., 86.

7. Shine Louise Houston, Reddit IAmA, June 17, 2015, https://www.
reddit.com/r/IAmA/comments/3a6gol/im_shine_louise_hous-
ton_an_awardwinning_porn/?sort=new.

8. The following comes from Jiz Lee, personal email correspon-
dence to the author, November 1, 2010.

9. Lynn Comella, "Film Professor Constance Penley on Sex, Education
. . . and Sex Education," *Las Vegas Weekly*, November 7, 2012, http://
www.lasvegasweekly.com/news/2012/nov/07/film-professor-
constance-penley-sex-education-and-/. See also Constance Penley,
"A Feminist Teaching Pornography? That's Like Scopes Teaching
Evolution!" in *The Feminist Porn Book: The Politics of Producing
Pleasure*, ed. Tristan Taormino et al. (New York: The Feminist Press,
2013), 179–199; and "Truth Claims About Porn: When Dogma
and Data Collide" in *The Philosophy of Pornography: Contemporary
Perspectives*, ed. Lindsay Coleman and Jacob M. Held (Lanham,
MD: Rowman & Littlefield, 2014).

10. Lindsay Coleman and Jacob M. Held, "Introduction: Why
Pornography?" in *The Philosophy of Pornography: Contemporary
Perspectives*, ed. Lindsay Coleman and Jacob M. Held (Lanham,
MD: Rowman & Littlefield, 2014), xi–xvi.

11. Comella, "Film Professor Constance Penley."

12. Quoted in Shira Tarrant, "Pornography and Pedagogy: Teaching
Media Literacy," in *New Views on Pornography: Sexuality, Politics,
and the Law*, ed. Lynn Comella and Shira Tarrant (Santa Barbara,
CA: Praeger, 2015), 422.

13. Mireille Miller-Young, "The Pedagogy of Pornography: Teaching
Hardcore Media in a Feminist Studies Classroom," *Signs* 2, no. 2
(Fall 2010), http://ffc.twu.edu/issue_2-2/miller-young_essay_1_
2-2.html.

14. Erika Lust, "How Virtual Reality Could Change Porn for the
Better," *Fortune*, July 29, 2015, http://fortune.com/2015/07/29/
virtual-reality-porn/.

# SUGGESTED READINGS

Boyle, Karen, ed. *Everyday Pornography*. New York: Routledge, 2010.

Bronstein, Carolyn. *Battling Pornography: The American Feminist Anti-Pornography Movement, 1976–1986*. New York: Cambridge University Press, 2011.

Coleman, Lyndsay and Jacob M. Held, eds. *The Philosophy of Pornography: Contemporary Perspectives*. Boulder, CO: Rowman & Littlefield, 2014.

Comella, Lynn and Shira Tarrant, eds. *New Views on Pornography: Sexuality, Politics, and the Law*. Santa Barbara, CA: Praeger, 2015.

Dean, Tim, Steven Ruszczycky, and David Squires, eds. *Porn Archives*. Durham, NC: Duke University Press, 2014.

Dines, Gail. *Pornland: How Porn Has Hijacked Our Sexuality*. Boston: Beacon Press, 2010.

Duggan, Lisa and Nan D. Hunter. *Sex Wars: Sexual Dissent and Political Culture*. New York: Routledge, 2006.

Dworkin, Andrea. *Pornography: Men Possessing Women*. New York: Perigee, 1981.

Escoffier, Jeffrey. *Bigger Than Life: The History of Gay Porn Cinema from Beefcake to Hardcore*. Philadelphia: Running Press, 2009.

Grebowicz, Margret. *Why Internet Porn Matters*. Stanford, CA: Stanford University Press, 2013.

Jensen, Robert. *Getting Off: Pornography and the End of Masculinity*. Cambridge, MA: South End Press, 2007.

Kipnis, Laura. *Bound and Gagged: Pornography and the Politics of Fantasy in America*. Durham, NC: Duke University Press, 1998.

Lee, Jiz, ed. *Coming Out Like a Porn Star: Essays on Pornography, Protection, and Privacy*. Los Angeles: ThreeL Media, 2015.

McNair, Brian. *Porno? Chic! How Pornography Changed the World and Made It a Better Place*. New York: Routledge, 2013.

Miller-Young, Mireille. *A Taste for Brown Sugar: Black Women in Pornography*. Durham, NC: Duke University Press, 2014.

Nash, Jennifer Christine. *The Black Body in Ecstasy: Reading Race, Reading Pornography*. Durham, NC: Duke University Press, 2014.

Nathan, Debbie. *Pornography*. Toronto: Groundwood Books, 2007.

Paasonen, Susanna. *Carnal Resonance: Affect and Online Pornography*. Cambridge, MA: MIT Press, 2011.

Sabo, Anne G. *After Pornified: How Women Are Transforming Pornography and Why It Really Matters*. Winchester: UK, 2012.

Strossen, Nadine. *Defending Pornography: Free Speech, Sex, and the Fight for Women's Rights*. New York: New York University Press, 2000.

Strub, Whitney. *Perversion for Profit: The Politics of Pornography and the Rise of the New Right*. New York: Columbia University Press, 2011.

Sullivan, Rebecca and Alan McKee. *Pornography: Structures, Agency and Performance*. Cambridge, UK: Polity, 2015.

Taormino, Tristan, Celine Parreñas Shimuzu, Constance Penley, and Mireille Miller-Young, eds. *The Feminist Porn Book: The Politics of Producing Pleasure*. New York: The Feminist Press, 2013.

Vance, Carole S., ed. *Pleasure and Danger: Exploring Female Sexuality*. London: Pandora, 1989.

Williams, Linda, ed. *Porn Studies*. Durham, NC: Duke University Press, 2004.

# INDEX

H 8/16